INTERNATIONAL DEVELOPMENT IN FOCUS

Braced for Impact

Reforming Kazakhstan's National Financial Holding for Development Effectiveness and Market Creation

MARTIN MELECKY, PASQUALE DI BENEDETTA, ISMAEL AHMAD FONTAN, GANBAATAR JAMBAL, AND MICHEL NOEL

WORLD BANK GROUP

Contents

Boxes

Figures

Tables

Preface

The government of Kazakhstan has embarked on an ambitious journey to reform its quasi-fiscal sector. As in many other countries, the quasi-fiscal sector in Kazakhstan is large and complex and includes numerous state-owned enterprises (SOEs) and other public legal entities. In 2022, more than 6,000 SOEs were owned by the central or local governments—with about 10 percent incorporated as joint stock companies or limited liability partnerships. Quasi-public entities were established in different legal forms and are present across various sectors of the economy, including energy, transportation and communications, financial services, health care and education, utilities, and research and training. The largest SOEs are owned by holding companies that manage them on behalf of the state. Examples of the holding companies are the sovereign wealth fund Samruk Kazyna for state-owned industrial assets, the national medical holding company for SOEs in the health sector, KazAgroFinance for SOEs in agriculture (KazAgro's subsidiaries have been merged under Baiterek Holding), and Baiterek Holding for state-owned financial institutions (SOFIs).

Baiterek Holding is a conglomerate of eight SOFIs whose consolidated balance sheets amounted to about 12 percent of Kazakhstan's gross domestic product in 2022. These SOFIs run both wholesale and retail operations to support development in the country. They vary in type and include state commercial financial institutions, development finance institutions (DFIs), intermediaries of state financial subsidies, and other fiscal agent functions. For instance, they cover more than 40 percent of bank lending to small and medium enterprises, close to 70 percent of residential mortgage lending, and more than 90 percent of agricultural lending and leasing. Baiterek's impact at the level of beneficiaries, including enterprises, households, and communities, as well as at the level of financial market creation has been criticized by stakeholders. Reforming Baiterek Holding is, therefore, a priority of the quasi-fiscal sector reform.

This book aims to fill a gap in the literature on DFIs and impact investing by introducing a novel framework that assesses DFIs and DFI conglomerates against benchmarks for impact, capital, risk, and governance and applying it to the case of Kazakhstan's national financial holding company, Baiterek. This publication aims to support the reform efforts of the government of Kazakhstan by offering policy options and technical recommendations for Baiterek that could be used in the formulation of an action plan. If the government commits to a sufficiently comprehensive set of top-down and bottom-up actions, implementing the plan could help Baiterek advance among the leading DFIs globally.

State financial support programs in many developing countries urgently need consolidation and strengthening of their institutional setups to become impactful development finance programs. Some countries are already on the same path as Kazakhstan, building DFI conglomerates to enhance governance of state financial support programs and better deliver on impact. Kazakhstan's experience with assessing its DFI conglomerate against the novel impact-capital-risk-governance framework could thus be informative for other countries. It could guide similar assessments, help consolidate countries' SOFI space into clear commercial SOFIs and a DFI structure with double bottom line objectives, or help countries build a new DFI structure from weakly institutionalized and governed state financial support programs. Furthermore, it could help countries strengthen impact frameworks to include both ultimate beneficiaries and market creation; help them select investment projects based on the economic rate of return, hurdle rate, and appropriate level of concessionality; or help them holistically manage the risk that DFIs assume across financial, operational, and impact-related risks (such as just-transition risk).

Acknowledgments

This report was prepared by a team led by Martin Melecky (lead economist) and including Pasquale Di Benedetta (senior financial sector specialist), Ismael Ahmad Fontan (senior financial sector specialist), Ganbaatar Jambal (senior financial sector specialist), and Michel Noel (senior consultant). The report was prepared under the direction of Tatiana Proskuryakova (country director), Asad Alam (regional director), Ilias Skamnelos (practice manager), and Andrei Mikhnev (country manager).

For their guidance, support, and comments, the team would like to thank Jean-Francois Marteau (practice manager and former country manager for Kazakhstan), Jane Olga Ebinger (program leader), Salamat Kussainova (governance specialist), Kanat Kaiyrberli (senior country officer), Mariana Iootty De Paiva Dias (senior economist), Andrei Busuioc (senior financial management specialist), Katerina Levitanskaya (International Finance Corporation [IFC] operations officer), Gaukhar Ospanova (private sector specialist), Asset Bizhan (private sector specialist), Alexander Berg (senior financial sector specialist), Wei-Jen Leow (senior environmental finance specialist), Sjamsu Rahardja (senior economist), and Galina Klimenko (IFC principal investment officer). For their support with matters related to administration and communication, the team is grateful to Gulmira Akshatyrova (program assistant), Aisulu Mailybayeva (executive assistant), Aigerim Alpkarina (program assistant), and Shynar Jetpissova (external affairs officer).

This report would not have been possible without the kind assistance and help provided by counterparts from the Kazakhstan Ministry of National Economy and Baiterek Holding and its subsidiaries, and the team would like to express sincere gratitude to Alibek Kuantyrov (minister of national economy); Zhadyra Temirbayeva (director, Ministry of National Economy); Altair Akhmetov (head of the Department of Public Administration, Administration of the President of the Republic of Kazakhstan); Zhomart Abiessov (deputy head of the Department of Public Administration, Administration of the President of the Republic of Kazakhstan); Almaz Abylkassymov (deputy head of the Department of Public Administration, Administration of the President of the Republic of Kazakhstan); Kanat Sharlapayev (former chairman of the board, Baiterek; current minister of industry and construction); Madina Yerzhanova (head of Department of Strategy and Analytics, Baiterek); Asset Tazhikenov (director,

Project Management Department, Baiterek); Kalzhan Argynbay (senior manager, Project Management Department, Baiterek); Botagoz Abisheva (deputy CEO, Development Bank of Kazakhstan [DBK]); Marat Yelibaev (chief client officer, DBK); Adina Berikkyzy (director, Funding and International Relations, DBK); Arsen Mustafin (director, Loan Programs Department, Entrepreneurship Development Fund [DAMU]); and Nursultan Abykaev (director, Portfolio Funds Department, Qazaqstan Investment Corporation [QIC]).

The findings, interpretations, and conclusions expressed in this report are those of the World Bank staff and do not necessarily reflect the views of the Executive Board of the World Bank or the governments they represent. For information about the World Bank and its activities in Kazakhstan, please visit https://www.worldbank.org/en/country/kazakhstan.

About the Authors

Ismael Ahmad Fontan is senior financial sector specialist in the Financial Sector Advisory Center (FinSAC) of the Finance, Competitiveness and Innovation Global Practice of the World Bank. He specializes in banking regulation, supervision, resolution, and sustainability. Ismael joined the World Bank in 2019 and has worked in many countries across Southeastern and Eastern Europe, the South Caucasus, Central Asia, East Asia, and Africa. Before joining the World Bank, Ismael worked in the Banking Supervision and Regulation Departments of the Bank of Spain and held senior positions in consulting businesses (PwC and Bluecap Management Consulting). He has a degree in law and business administration from ICADE.

Pasquale Di Benedetta is senior financial sector specialist at the World Bank and specializes in corporate governance reforms for capital markets, financial sectors, and state enterprises. He has worked for the World Bank and the International Monetary Fund in more than 60 countries for over 15 years. An Italian national, Pasquale earned his international law degree in Italy (Bari and Trento) and Austria (Salzburg) and his master's degree in the United States (Johns Hopkins University). He is fluent in Italian, English, and Spanish.

Ganbaatar Jambal is senior financial sector specialist with the Finance, Competitiveness and Innovation Global Practice of the World Bank, Europe and Central Asia Unit. He specializes in banking supervision, risk management, economic modeling, and green finance. Ganbaatar joined the World Bank in 2015 and since then has worked on development projects in the Europe and Central Asia, East Asia and Pacific, and Africa regions. Before joining the World Bank, Ganbaatar held various senior-level positions at the Central Bank of Mongolia, including director of regulation policy division, director general of banking supervision, chief economist, senior adviser to the governor of the central bank, and chairman of the National Coordination Committee on Anti–Money Laundering. He holds a master's degree in financial economics for public policy and a doctorate in economics.

Martin Melecky is lead economist in the Finance, Competitiveness and Innovation Global Practice of the World Bank. He has led financial sector assessment programs, development policy operations, and investment and technical assistance projects in South Asia, Emerging Europe, and Central Asia. Martin has coauthored regional reports on hidden debt in South Asia, economic corridors in South Asia, and finance for shared prosperity in Europe and Central Asia. He is also the lead author of the chapter in the 2014 *World Development Report* on the role of the financial system in risk management. Martin has published in a range of journals (*Journal of Development Economics; World Bank Economic Review; World Bank Research Observer; Cambridge Journal of Regions, Economy and Society; Journal of Regional Science; Journal of Banking and Finance; Journal of Financial Stability; Journal of International Money and Finance;* and *Climate Change Economics*). A Czech national, he received a PhD in economics from the University of New South Wales, Australia.

Michel Noel is senior consultant at the World Bank, where he advises teams on the reform of the legal and regulatory framework for private equity and venture capital and on the development and implementation of hybrid public-private investment funds, including green and blue funds across several regions. He has held a range of technical and managerial positions during his career at the World Bank from 1980 to 2017 and has published widely on financial sector reform and privatization. He was practice manager for nonbank financial institutions from 2009 to 2015 and head of investment funds from 2015 to 2017 at the Finance, Competitiveness and Innovation Global Practice of the World Bank. He is cofounder and managing partner of Sovereign Fund Advisory LLC and senior adviser at Bloccelerate Venture Capital. He holds a master's degree in economics and social sciences from the University of Namur, Belgium.

Executive Summary

Baiterek, a state-owned holding company that controls development finance institutions (DFIs) incorporated in Kazakhstan, has grown into a large financial support tool of the Kazakhstani government, one that influences the financing of nonextractive economic sectors and the workings of financial markets. Baiterek's total consolidated assets as a share of gross domestic product grew from 5.6 percent in 2013, the year Baiterek was established, to about 12 percent in 2022. Baiterek plays a dual role as both a DFI and a fiscal agent—that is, it intermediates state budget funds for financial service subsidies and purchases bonds of subnational entities.

Despite its dominant role and reported influence, Baiterek may not be meeting its potential to credibly deliver development impacts, create efficient financial markets, or mobilize private capital. The holding company aims to deliver positive impacts to end-beneficiaries—that is, micro, small, and medium enterprises and households—by contributing to increases in sales and helping to generate jobs among beneficiaries. However, Baiterek's methodology for measuring impact lacks credible attribution and is compromised by double or triple counting of "impact." Furthermore, Baiterek lacks a clear focus on financial market creation and additionality in terms of capital mobilization at transaction and funding levels.

Although proactive in promoting the environmental, social, and governance agenda, Baiterek could help the economy and financial markets tackle mitigation and adaptation challenges by including climate finance and green impacts in its strategy. Baiterek's strategy and impact framework could center on delivering climate impacts at the level of beneficiaries, as well as on deepening the green finance markets. Although green finance is a recent area of focus for the DFI industry, Baiterek could become a leading institution in this area globally.

Baiterek's dual role as DFI and fiscal agent creates numerous tensions in governing the holding company to achieve credible medium-term impacts. By competing directly in financial markets on unequal terms, Baiterek may create distortions and crowd out private capital—specifically prevent it from entering markets or scaling up its provision of some financial services. Relatedly, the existing governance setup for Baiterek does not help foster political independence in financing decisions, holistic risk management, or accountability for impacts.

The current report's assessment of and recommendations for Baiterek can be captured in a framework centered on impact, capital, risk, and governance.

Impact. Impact encompasses the medium-term outcomes at the level of both end-beneficiaries (firms, households) and the financial markets. Baiterek could develop a strategy for credible impacts at both levels. It could change the perception of operating under a "state forever" model in its interaction with financial markets and better crowd in private capital. Managing for credible impact involves four aspects: contribution, attribution, measurement, and verification. Furthermore, project selection could be improved by using a cost-benefit analysis targeting additionality in wider economic benefits such as jobs, value added, greenhouse gas emissions reduction, and resilience to shocks and disasters based on proper counterfactuals.

Capital. Capital management involves mobilizing more private capital and protecting both government and private funding from excessive losses. Mobilizing more private capital to fund Baiterek and its subsidiaries not only would leverage more funds for the Sustainable Development Goals but could also improve impact delivery and risk management through the stewardship of active investors. Although Baiterek has been tapping the bond markets for debt, it has not attracted equity investment. At the level of its project financing, Baiterek could follow the example of best international practice and include targets for private capital multipliers. From another perspective, contingent fiscal liabilities from Baiterek's financial leverage need to be explicitly managed within a medium-term debt management framework. Privatizations or nationalizations could create contingent liabilities and require a more transparent framework on decisions and pricing—in part to keep financial markets informed and manage their expectations.

Risk. Risk considerations cover the management of financial risks, enterprise risks, and risks related to impact. Managing financial and broader enterprise risks is essential for financial institutions such as Baiterek and its subsidiaries. The holding company has made good progress in many areas, but gaps remain. Baiterek could develop a framework for managing impact-related risks such as just-transition or displacement risks. A decentralized risk management model would be better aligned with Baiterek's activities than its current model and could hedge the group against political influence. In the decentralized model, the internal audit, chief risk officer, and chief compliance officer functions would be the main integrating lines for the risk oversight function at the Baiterek group level; this arrangement would reflect the best practice of the "three lines of defense" approach to risk management.

Governance. Governance comprises numerous aspects such as political independence, appropriate skills that match board and management responsibilities, and the accountability mechanism focused on impact. Under either the political or independent model for Baiterek's Board, various entities—Baiterek's management, the boards of Baiterek's subsidiaries, and the management of the subsidiaries—need to be duly isolated from political influence. These entities must also encompass diverse professional skills sets that cover the entire mandate of Baiterek—from commercial activities, to double bottom line financing, to provision of financial service subsidies. The current structure of the subsidiaries appears suboptimal and could be rationalized based on the business lines' commercial, double bottom line, and fiscal agent (efficient subsidy intermediation) objectives. In addition, Baiterek's accountability could be strengthened by improving the capacity of its enforcers and by adding new mechanisms for independent evaluation of medium-term impact, financial soundness, and market conduct. For the sake of Baiterek's DFI operations, the subsidy business line needs to be isolated and rationalized.

The recommendations made in this report could help the government of Kazakhstan prepare a detailed roadmap of well-sequenced actions that tackle the proposed reform agenda, indicate responsible entities, and include timelines for implementation. The government could adopt the technical recommendations and policy options as a group or could select only some based on political feasibility (see table O.1 for a summary of recommendations and appendix A for the detailed list).

The roadmap could encompass actions that tackle the reform agenda through both top-down and bottom-up approaches. Top-down approaches—such as policy reforms and legal and regulatory actions—are comprehensive but take longer to implement and are slower to effect change in the corporate culture. Therefore, complementary bottom-up actions are often used in change management to launch pilots that have demonstrative effects and change corporate culture from within. Such pilots could help create centers of excellence—professional drivers of change that generate positive spillovers throughout the organization. The pilots could include the development of innovative projects that leverage knowledge exchange and technical assistance from role model peers or multilateral development banks.

Abbreviations

3LoD	three lines of defense
ACC	Agrarian Credit Corporation
ACP	Asia Climate Partners
ADB	Asian Development Bank
AFR	Agency for Regulation and Development of the Financial Markets
AGO	Auditor General Office
AML/CFT	anti–money laundering and combating the financing of terrorism
ASPIR	Agency for Strategic Planning and Reforms
BNDES	Banco Nacional de Desenvolvimento (Brazil)
CDC	Caisse des Dépôts et Consignations (France)
CDP	Cassa Depositi e Prestiti (Italy)
CEO	chief executive officer
CPG	Commercialization and Privatization Group
CRO	chief risk officer
DAMU	Entrepreneurship Development Fund
DBK	Development Bank of Kazakhstan
DBSA	Development Bank of South Africa
DFI	development finance institution
ERR	economic rate of return
ESG	environmental, social, and governance
ESMS	environmental and social management system
FC4S	Financial Centres for Sustainability
GB	Grupo Bicentenario (Colombia)
GDP	gross domestic product
GEEREF	Global Energy Efficiency and Renewable Energy Fund
GHG	greenhouse gas
GIIN	Global Investment Impact Network

GVA	gross value added
HCGF	Housing Construction Guarantee Fund
IDD	integrity due diligence
IFI	international financial institution
IRR	internal rate of return
ISIF	Ireland Strategic Investment Fund
JSC	joint stock company
KASE	Kazakhstan Stock Exchange
KCM	Kazyna Capital Management
KHC	Kazakhstan Housing Company
KPI	key performance indicator
LEA	local executive authority
MHCP	Ministerio de Hacienda y Crédito Público (Colombia)
MNE	Ministry of National Economy
MSME	micro, small, and medium enterprise
MTEF	medium-term expenditure framework
NBK	National Bank of Kazakhstan
NGO	nongovernmental organization
ODA	official development assistance
OECD	Organisation for Economic Co-operation and Development
PFI	participating financial institution
PLG	partial loan guarantee
QIC	Qazaqstan Investment Corporation
ROE	return on equity
SDG	Sustainable Development Goal
SFG	Strategic Finance Group
SIR	subsidized interest rates
SME	small and medium enterprise
SMFAC	Subsidy Management and Fiscal Agency Corporation
SOE	state-owned enterprise
SOFI	state-owned financial institution

€	euro
R$	real
Rub	ruble
T	tenge
US$	US dollar

Overview

INTRODUCTION

Baiterek Holding, a state-owned holding company that controls development finance institutions (DFIs) in Kazakhstan, has become a giant financial support tool of the government that directly affects the financing of the local economy and the functioning of financial markets. Baiterek's total (consolidated) assets as a share of gross domestic product (GDP) grew from 5.6 percent in 2013, the year Baiterek was established, to about 12 percent in 2022. Baiterek plays a dual role as a DFI and a fiscal agent—that is, it intermediates state budget funds for financial service subsidies and finances bonds of subnational entities. Baiterek's intermediation of subsidies funded annually from the government budget might add a couple of percentage points to GDP if properly reported. Baiterek dominates and directs several segments of the financial market. For example, Baiterek's KazAgroFinance subsidiary is practically the sole provider of agricultural leasing in Kazakhstan. Through another subsidiary, the Entrepreneurship Development Fund (DAMU), Baiterek influences 40–50 percent of the total bank lending to small and medium enterprises (SMEs) in Kazakhstan. Moreover, Baiterek's Otbasy Bank is the leading provider of (subsidized) retail mortgage loans in Kazakhstan. Despite its enormous size, Baiterek does not figure explicitly in national or financial sector strategies. As a result, its objectives, key performance indicators (KPIs), and targets need to be negotiated through a complex and lengthy process that impedes efficiency, transparency, and accountability in its operations.

Compared to its potential, Baiterek may be falling short in delivering credible impacts for ultimate beneficiaries, creating efficient financial markets, and mobilizing private capital. Baiterek aims to deliver positive impacts at the level of final beneficiary (micro, small, and medium enterprise [MSME], household) primarily by helping beneficiaries increase sales and jobs. However, Baiterek's methodology for measuring impact is weak because it lacks credible attribution—notably, it does not consider counterfactuals—and is compromised by double or triple counting of "impact." For example, if the Agrarian Credit Corporation (ACC) provides an interest subsidy to agribusiness and, at the same time, the agribusiness benefits from a credit guarantee by DAMU, both ACC and DAMU would take credit for the increase in jobs at the agribusiness. Neither subsidiary would account for how the average agribusiness in Kazakhstan or its peer region grew. Nor would ACC or DAMU adjust its impact estimate by the size of its respective nonmarket support (or even simply divide the estimate by two). The impact reported by Baiterek is thus not credible in the eyes of many stakeholders. Moreover, Baiterek does not sufficiently consider how its actions impact financial market development; it often crowds out private capital from financial service providers to end-users, such as in mortgage lending or agricultural leasing. Baiterek may also distort financial markets through large, untargeted subsidies; such subsidies might have contributed to stagnation in the MSME lending market in the past 10 years. Finally, although Baiterek was able to issue bonds in local and global markets and mobilize financing from several global institutional investors, it has so far not attracted private equity participation in its various business lines, limiting its ability to benefit from additionality in accountability and stewardship. The only exceptions are funds sponsored by the Qazaqstan Investment Corporation (QIC), which is Baiterek's subsidiary focused on the private equity/venture capital market;[1] however, the domestic part of this market has not been developing successfully.

Climate finance and green impacts could be highlighted in Baiterek's impact strategy to help the economy and financial markets tackle the green economy transition and adaptation challenges. Currently, Baiterek's impact strategy and framework do not sufficiently address green mitigation and adaptation either at the level of beneficiaries (firms and households) or at the level of financial market deepening. Although the green economy is a recent area of focus for the DFI industry, Baiterek could become one of the leading institutions in this area globally. Baiterek should be commended for its nascent environmental, social, and governance (ESG) efforts, but even if completed, the ESG approaches being pursued typically fall short of what DFI investing for credible green impacts requires (see more detailed discussion of impact, capital, risk, and governance later in this section). Baiterek's next step could be a credible greening of its main products on a pilot basis—such as large project financing, credit guarantee provision, leasing, or equity funds sponsoring—before developing a comprehensive green impact framework. Furthermore, while the provision of export insurance and agricultural insurance are well acknowledged and welcome, Baiterek could also prioritize the development of the private catastrophe insurance industry in Kazakhstan among its sectoral interventions; this step would help finance climate change adaptation and resilience. Other progressive interventions to support the financing of the risks from climate-induced disasters could include sponsoring a national reinsurance pool or promoting catastrophe bond issuance for Kazakhstan.

The dual role of Baiterek as both DFI and fiscal agent creates numerous tensions in governing the holding company to achieve credible impacts over the medium term. The DFI function of Baiterek and its subsidiaries is reflected on the consolidated balance sheet. It covers mainly the intermediation of funding from equity and debt contributions to end-beneficiaries through (private) financial institutions participating in Baiterek's programs, including the "fund of funds" structures sponsored by QIC as a partner in public-private equity funds. There is also one fiscal agent function reflected on Baiterek's balance sheet: the purchase of local executive authority (LEA) bonds, which may reflect and try to mend the shortfall of the subnational/municipal fiscal framework.[2] Most importantly, there are large subsidies that Baiterek intermediates to support access to financial services annually for the state; this activity is funded from the government budget. The KPIs and targets for these subsidies are negotiated by individual ministries—outside what could be labeled the medium-term impact framework related to the DFI function of Baiterek—based on their (perceived) ownership of the funding and expected results. These negotiations are complex and protracted. For example, the process for setting KPIs for 2019 budget funding commitments started in November 2019 and ended in November 2021— meaning that Baiterek effectively operated without a KPI framework and targets during that period. Moreover, ministries sometimes commit funding for negotiated subsidy programs and their KPI targets, then do not deliver the full amount of funding—yet still demand that Baiterek deliver on its part of the deal. Overall, the fiscal agent role and intermediation of annual fiscal subsidies exposes Baiterek to political distortions, decreases the political independence of the DFI function required by best international practice, and weakens Baiterek's potential for functioning as an efficient DFI (conglomerate).

By competing directly in financial markets on advantageous terms, Baiterek might be creating distortions and crowding out private capital—preventing it from entering markets or scaling up its provision of some financial services. There is also the important question of Baiterek's structure, specifically its mix of Tier 1 (wholesale) and Tier 2 (direct market participant) operations. Currently, the direct provision of credit by Otbasy and ACC (and its daughter KazAgroFinance) together with the acquired (nationalized) Bereke Bank (formerly Sberbank Kazakhstan) could account for one-third to one-half of Baiterek's operations. The market is signaling that Otbasy is crowding out banks from providing mortgage lending to viable clients; that KazAgroFinance has monopolized agricultural leasing in the country; and that the equity funds controlled by QIC (as owner or general partner) have not robustly aided the development of local private equity/venture capital industry. There is no economic rationale for Baiterek to maintain a direct presence and compete in the commercial markets with privately owned financial firms. Rather, Baiterek could enter segments or niches with reliably established market failures and help the private market grow into those niches—including by risk sharing in transactions—and then exit based on pre-agreed sunset triggers. Many stakeholders perceive in Baiterek's operations a "state forever" approach that is not helping the economy grow productively or promoting efficiency or accountability in spending of fiscal resources.

The current governance arrangements for Baiterek do not appear to shield investment decisions, holistic risk management, or accountability for development impacts from political interference. Baiterek's Board of Directors is largely political, chaired by the prime minister.[3] This arrangement may be substandard according to the Organisation for Economic Co-operation and Development (OECD) guidance for state-owned enterprise (SOE) board composition and independence. The board of directors could serve as a vehicle for effectively conducting the ownership function and providing coordinated strategic guidance on behalf of the government. For this model to work, however, Baiterek's management, subsidiary boards of directors, and subsidiary management would need to be fully politically independent—which they are not at present. Alternatively, Baiterek could adopt the governance model recently adopted by Samruk Kazyna, the holding company for SOEs in Kazakhstan, which entails political independence for the board of directors, or it could seek an even more independent model. Currently, decisions on subsidiaries' large projects and programs and on credit risk underwriting are not properly insulated from possible political influence; this arrangement could be the most pressing governance issue, especially for the Development Bank of Kazakhstan (DBK). An independent corporate audit function running through the holding company and its subsidiaries, with independent reporting to the board, has not been ascertained so far. Board impact committees at the levels of the holding company and its subsidiaries are currently missing but, if established, could help promote the delivery of credible medium-term impact. The function of the chief risk officer (CRO), including independent reporting on integrated risk management to the management teams and the boards, could help—in part by managing just-transition risks or crowding-out risks. The main accountability framework—working through the ownership function performed by a Ministry of National Economy (MNE) directorate and the Parliamentary Committee on Finance and Economics in conjunction with the Auditor General Office (AGO)—appears weak, notably regarding its attention to medium-term impacts. Hence, the overall structure of checks and balances does not decisively propel Baiterek toward delivering credible impact via the provision of financial services through private markets or toward assuming maximum fiscal responsibility.

The assessments and recommendations offered in this report can be captured in a framework centered on impact, capital, risk, and governance (figure O.1). Impact encompasses the medium-term outcomes—as opposed to outputs (loans granted)—at the level of end-beneficiaries (firms, households) and financial markets that Baiterek interacts with and that it should share risk with for market development purposes. Capital involves mobilizing private capital to cofinance Baiterek's operations to promote development impacts, as well as protecting the capital entrusted by government and private markets from excessive (unexpected) financial losses. Capital also involves an overall frugal approach to using fiscal resources, including for interest rate subsidies. Risk considerations cover the management of financial risks in line with international standards for financial conglomerates, various enterprise risks, and (especially important for DFIs) risks related to impact delivery—such as just-transition risks or crowding-out risks in markets or locations.[4] Governance comprises numerous aspects; some of the most important for Baiterek include the political independence of decision-making on the financing of projects and programs, the appropriate range and

FIGURE O.1

Report framework: Impact, capital, risk, and governance

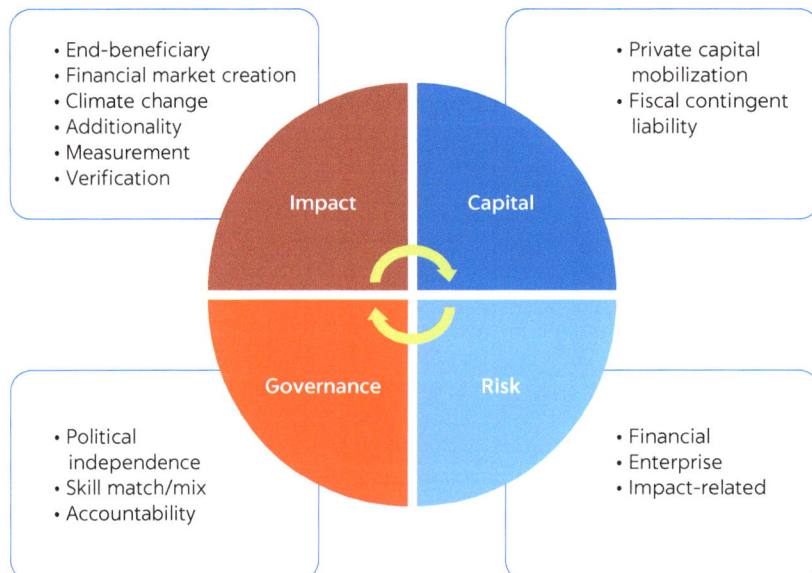

- End-beneficiary
- Financial market creation
- Climate change
- Additionality
- Measurement
- Verification

Impact

- Private capital mobilization
- Fiscal contingent liability

Capital

Governance

- Political independence
- Skill match/mix
- Accountability

Risk

- Financial
- Enterprise
- Impact-related

Source: World Bank.

diversity of skills among boards and management to ensure they can meet their responsibilities, and an accountability mechanism focused on the impact that can truly challenge boards and management to deliver on their mandate. These framework components are discussed in the following sections.

IMPACT

Credible impact strategy centers on delivering impacts, not only at the level of end-beneficiaries but also at the level of financial markets, whose development Baiterek should support. The impact strategy could be a self-standing document or a part of Baiterek's strategy statements covering four to five years. Over this period, the impact committees of both the Baiterek Board and subsidiary boards would guide, monitor, and assess the performance on impact using their professional skills and diverse experience in managing for development impact. The impact strategy—and more broadly, Baiterek Holding's mandate and policy implementation role—should be aligned with the national development strategy and the strategy for the development of financial markets.[5] The document should state the objectives, KPIs, and their targets to be met by the end of the four- to five-year period at both the beneficiary level and the financial market level. For example, for beneficiaries in entrepreneurship, the KPIs could include an increase in value added or jobs and a reduction in greenhouse gas (GHG) emissions. For large infrastructure projects, impact KPIs could include wider economic benefits related to local job creation, value added per worker (productivity), GHG emission reduction, or independently certified increases in infrastructure resilience. For housing finance, impact KPIs could include access to sanitary housing with certified energy efficiency and resilience, offered on sustainable financial terms (measured by debt-service-to-income ratio). Concerning impact on the creation of financial markets, Baiterek and DAMU could, for example, aim to sustainably increase MSME financing as a share of total lending by the institutions participating in their programs and by the banking and nonbank credit industries at large (figure O.2). Another goal could be to increase mortgage lending by participating financial institutions that support access to energy-efficient and resilient housing

FIGURE O.2

Baiterek's contribution to total SME lending

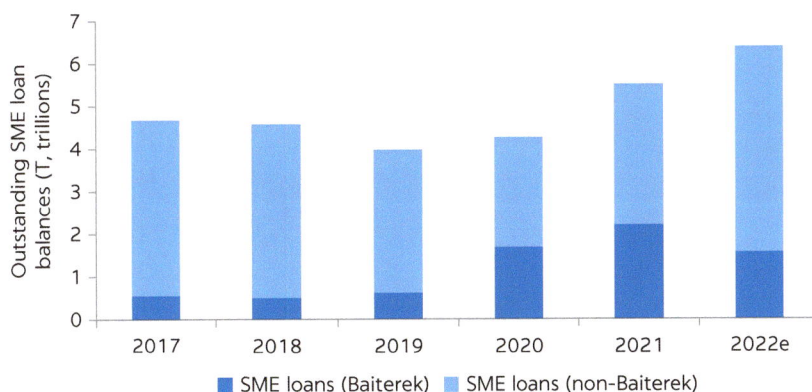

Sources: Baiterek National Management Holding JSC; Agency for Regulation and Development of the Financial Markets.
Note: 2022 numbers are estimated. SME = small and medium enterprise; non-Baiterek = SME loans by banks not affiliated with Baiterek Holding.

for all viable borrowers (figure O.3).[6] Yet another goal could be to ensure that infrastructure financing can grow with the support of syndication and/or offshore investor participation or with regulatory supporting factors backed up by guarantees as applicable. Following some best-practice international examples, such as that offered by the Global Energy Efficiency and Renewable Energy Fund (GEEREF), Baiterek Holding or its selected subsidiaries could introduce targets for private capital multipliers.

Managing for credible impact involves addressing four aspects: contribution, attribution, measurement, and verification. Baiterek and its subsidiaries need to clearly communicate how their various interventions/products contribute to positive impacts (theory of change)—for example, how DAMU's loan guarantee program for lending to SMEs can improve SMEs' access to private market financing. In addition, Baiterek needs a measurement methodology that accurately attributes results among various products or controls for other factors, such as simultaneous opening of export markets that increase SMEs' access to supply chain financing. For monitoring, peer group counterfactuals and their trends could be a practical approach. Rigorous ex post impact evaluation of Baiterek's interventions could include quasi-experimental approaches (such as the difference-in-differences method) or the synthetic control method (using a regression setup to account for confounding factors or a possible selection bias). Third-party verification of monitoring and evaluation are crucial aspects for establishing the credibility of impacts. Verification of monitored impact measures could be audited and disclosed annually by independent auditors, credit rating companies, or specialized licensed firms. Such market verification channels are best funded independently—for example, from the fees of end-beneficiaries or participating financial institutions paid into a verification fund. Evaluations need to be commissioned and conducted independently from Baiterek. One approach proposed in the report is for AGO or the Agency for Strategic Planning and Reforms (ASPIR) to commission an evaluation by a reputable international university or think tank.

Investment decisions and project selection are yet other management tasks that require rigor and use of a cost-benefit analysis to account for targeted wider

FIGURE O.3

Otbasy Bank's share in housing loans

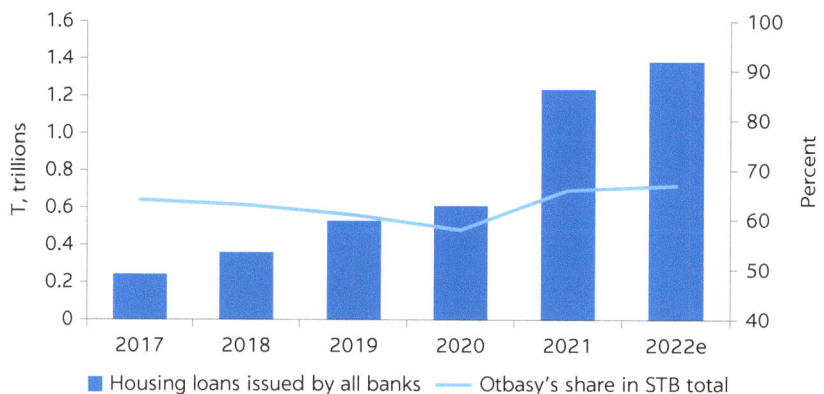

Sources: Baiterek National Management Holding JSC; Otbasy Bank; Agency for Regulation and Development of the Financial Markets.
Note: 2022 numbers are estimated. STB = second-tier bank.

economic benefits (Eliasson and Lundberg 2012; Florio, Morretta, and Willak 2018; Mishan and Quah 2020). Based on its established contribution to advancing its goals, Baiterek needs project selection methodologies for large projects and programs, including a flagging system of indicators for selection of small projects under large programs. An improved selection methodology should also apply to back-to-back funding of large projects and programs, including funding through green bond issuance and the allocation of their proceeds to financing of green-impact investments. Specifically, based on its impact framework, Baiterek could define the framework for the cost-benefit analysis that helps identify costs and benefits and also establish a timeline over which impact is managed. In addition, the wider economic benefits and costs of Baiterek's intervention versus the status quo could be valued in currency terms. That is, Baiterek could establish the value of a created job and use established benchmarks for the carbon price, while for value added the existing monetary value could be used.[7] Appropriate discount factor(s) would then be applied to calculate the net present value of the net benefits and the economic rate of return (ERR). In case of multiple KPIs, either the highest ERR should be selected across the KPIs, or the ERRs should be summed to account for trade-offs and synergies (positive and negative covariances among the expected KPI values).[8] Maximizing the ERR of investments is subject to some minimum internal rate of return (IRR) ("hurdle rate")—either in absolute terms or linked to the yields of government bonds. Small projects under a large program that pass the hurdle rate and deliver a large enough ERR could be screened through a flagging system of indicators for selection developed under the program; this step would align each project selection with the ERR generation principles of the program. Figure O.4 summarizes the data inputs, measurement methodologies, and indicators at the investment selection, monitoring, and evaluation stages.

Learning from interventions and adjusting approaches and policies are inherent parts of successful impact delivery. The knowledge acquired and lessons learned through monitoring, impact evaluations, and holistic risk management can continuously inform the evolving approaches and design of Baiterek's support

FIGURE O.4

Data inputs, measurement methodologies, and indicators at the investment selection, monitoring, and evaluation stages

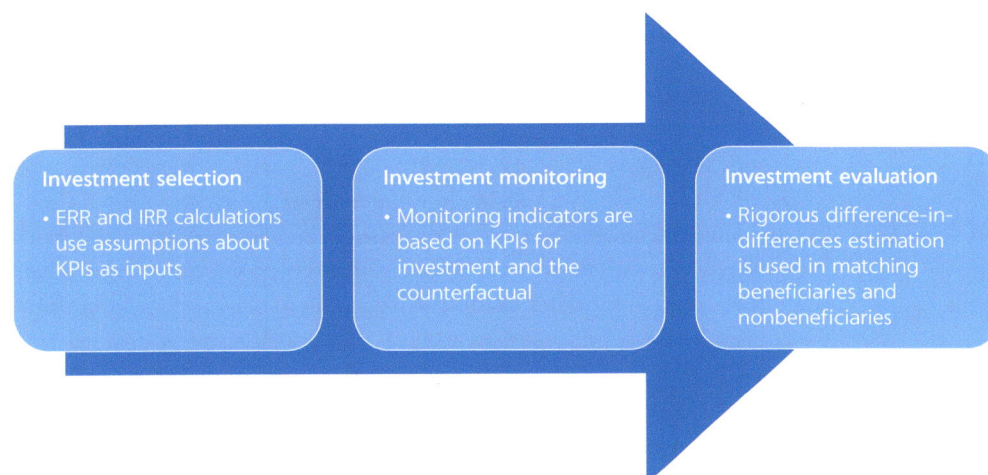

Source: World Bank.
Note: ERR = economic rate of return; IRR = internal rate of return; KPI = key performance indicator.

interventions, including their entry and phaseout. Timely action by Baiterek to adjust designs and delivery of financial support instruments is appropriate, and past mistakes should not be perceived as failures if they are corrected and the original designs were well intended. Taking informed risks and experimenting—by designing new pilots or evaluating, adjusting, scaling up, or phasing out different types of financial support—are required to properly calibrate financial support mechanisms to Kazakhstan's unique country context, business culture, and financial market needs. The impact committees of Baiterek Holding and subsidiaries could promote the exchange of information, intelligence, and knowledge on designing and delivering support for impact in the multifaceted context of Kazakhstan. They could encourage and reward informed experimentation and share experience on impact across instruments, subsidiaries, economic sectors, types of beneficiaries, and segments of financial markets. They could document their considerations, deliberations, and decisions and—to the extent allowed by confidentiality and governance arrangements—consider sharing them publicly and as part of South-South knowledge exchange.

CAPITAL

Mobilizing more private capital to fund Baiterek, including at the level of investment transactions, would not only support the billions-to-trillions agenda but also improve impact delivery and risk management. If Baiterek delivered credible impact, private investors with double bottom line objectives might wish to enter Baiterek through equity stakes. Private investment would further improve corporate governance and accountability, helping Baiterek scale up its impact—especially in greening the Kazakhstani economy, where scale is much needed. The positive influence of private equity stakes on Baiterek governance could be significant and help discipline through divestments in case Baiterek deviated from its impact framework or safeguards. International investors with larger stakes could bring accountability additionality through covenants, monitoring, and the credible threat of divestment if covenants were breached. Furthermore, active equity investors could exercise positive stewardship, including at the level of subsidiaries and especially if such entry led to privatization of a Baiterek subsidiary directly competing in the markets (at the Tier 2 level). Baiterek has been tapping the local and international bond markets for its funding, but the holders of its debt securities are not readily disclosed by Baiterek, making it hard for observers and other investors to understand the structure of the creditor pool or recognize funding from genuine private investors and their monitoring through covenants. The equity stakes of private investors remained zero as of early 2023.

Baiterek's function as a subsidy intermediator needs to be isolated, disciplined, and scaled down. The total amount of subsidies intermediated by Baiterek appears excessive and its effect on financial markets counterproductive, given the extent to which subsidies distort the incentives of market players. In many cases, the subsidies are not a one-time (or two-time) kick-starter to promote better access to finance, but rather as a social assistance measure, more suitable for granting through social assistance channels than through a DFI. Baiterek's annual negotiations with line ministries about subsidies and their KPIs and targets expose Baiterek to increased political interference and shocks—especially when committed subsidies are then not delivered in the full amount by the budget. The scaled-down subsidies to kick-start markets—lending to firms for green investments or access to finance for first-time borrowers without history—could be predictably managed and gradually withdrawn through the medium-term expenditure framework (MTEF) of the government. However, scaling down and disciplining subsidies is not enough for private investors to take a stake in Baiterek subsidiaries of interest. The investable subsidiaries need to be isolated from the subsidy intermediation functions, because investors do not like the political obligation and possible negative shocks the intermediation of subsidies entails. A more consolidated subsidiary structure could help Baiterek mobilize and protect capital at the subsidiary level by matching varying preferences of private capital and diversifying risks from individual business lines through their suitable pooling. The proposed approach for such isolation of subsidies is addressed in the later section on governance.

Fiscal contingent liabilities from possible Baiterek undercapitalization shocks could be more explicitly managed through a link to the medium-term debt management framework. Every quasi-fiscal institution (including financial SOEs) that is leveraged with debt can trigger fiscal contingent liabilities for the central government (Bova et al. 2016; Böwer 2017; Levy-Yeyati, Micco, and Panizza 2004; Melecky 2021). Baiterek Holding is no exception, with its leverage (debt-to-capital) ratio of about 5 to 1 in 2022. Accounting for fiscal contingent liabilities due to possible undercapitalization after various shocks is equally urgent if Baiterek or its subsidiaries are to be prudentially supervised as recommended. Such accounting, among other things, ensures the conditions of competitive neutrality relative to other financial institutions through a timely recapitalization, which is enforced by the financial regulator. Possible fiscal contingent liabilities could be managed through contingent fiscal reserves pooled across the quasi-fiscal sector (including through reserves in the sovereign wealth fund) and combined with enough space for contingent debt issuance or flexible dividend policy, including possible reduction in the generous dividend payouts to the government to start with. To help clarify the scope of possible fiscal contingent liabilities, Baiterek (and budget reporting) could disclose more transparently the flows of budget funds by purpose (subsidies, through-the-cycle versus emergency program funding, subnational purchases of bonds, and so on) as well as any agreed policy on netting of obligations or profit-and-loss accounts between Baiterek and the government.

Privatization or nationalization can also create contingent liabilities and require more transparent frameworks on decisions, timing, and pricing—to keep markets informed, among other reasons. Because some Baiterek subsidiaries or business lines may sooner or later be privatized—most urgently the nationalized Bereke Bank—fiscal contingent liabilities from the privatization (exit) contracts need to be captured sufficiently early in the medium-term debt management framework. This is because privatization contracts could involve various explicit or implicit guarantees that the acquiring investor might negotiate and also because the government's interest in keeping the privatized financial SOE a success might generate further support needs well after the privatization deal is closed.[9] Also, nationalization and acquisition of entities—such as the Bereke Bank—could potentially reveal pricing gaps at the privatization (exit) stage because of overoptimistic acquisition pricing. A policy for contingent liability management should be developed, in part to clarify whether Baiterek or the government (fiscal side) would be responsible for such contingent liabilities. The acquisitions and privatization deals need to be properly disclosed in terms of decisions, timing, and pricing, and the market—notably the current creditors and potential equity holders in Baiterek and its subsidiaries—needs to be properly informed.

RISK

Managing financial and broader enterprise risks is a core requirement for financial institutions such as Baiterek and its subsidiaries. The holding company is already focused on managing various financial risks following good international standards, but some potential weaknesses exist in relation to concentrated underwriting risks. For example, the DBK underwrites large projects, and the ultimate underwriting authority for large exposures rests with the DBK Board and by extension the Baiterek Board, which is mostly political. This arrangement creates a risk that the underwriting decisions could be politicized and not properly reflect the financial risks and returns or the impact (double bottom line objective) that DBK is responsible for delivering. DBK could thus originate significant risks for its and Baiterek's (consolidated) balance sheet. For example, large exposures of DBK represented more than 20 percent of Baiterek's total loans in 2021 (figure O.5). The large purchases of local executive bodies' bonds by the Kazakhstan Housing Company (KHC) in a context of a weak subnational/municipal fiscal framework could be another example. Net open foreign currency positions of several subsidiaries (figure O.6) are also affecting the risk profile of Baiterek. The broader enterprise risks faced by Baiterek related to managing and developing procedures include operational risk, anti–money laundering and combating the financing of terrorism (AML/CFT) risk (including for current and future creditors and potential investors), physical risk for business continuity stemming from natural and industrial hazards, and risks associated

FIGURE O.5

DBK's large exposures as a percentage of Baiterek's total loans, end-2021

percent

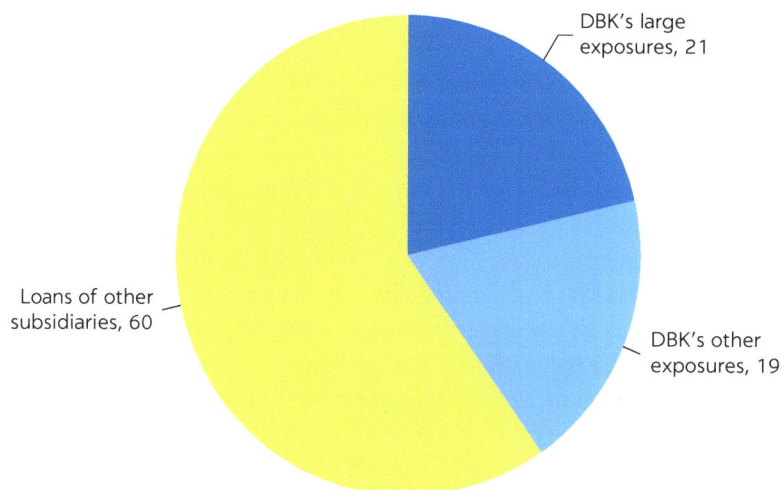

Sources: Baiterek National Management Holding JSC; Agency for Regulation and Development of the Financial Markets; National Bank of Kazakhstan.
Note: Large exposures of DBK include loans granted to eight companies, worth more than US$2.3 billion as of December 2021. DBK = Development Bank of Kazakhstan.

FIGURE O.6

Foreign currency net open position of selected Baiterek subsidiaries, end-2021

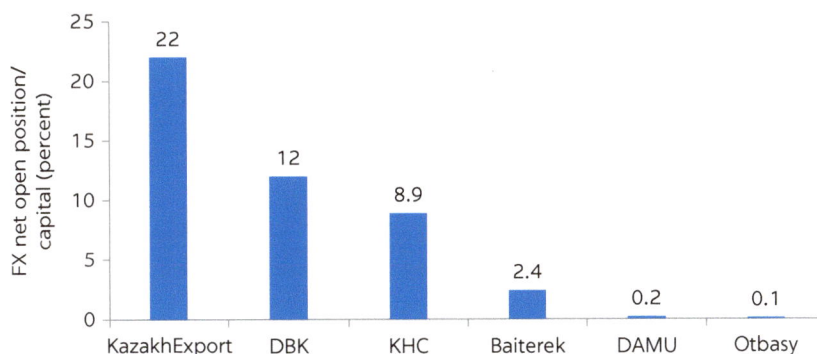

Source: Baiterek National Management Holding JSC.
Note: FX net open position is the sum of all open positions by individual foreign currencies. DAMU = Entrepreneurship Development Fund; DBK = Development Bank of Kazakhstan; KHC = Kazakhstan Housing Company.

with Baiterek's (excessive) environmental footprint, which could further trigger reputational risk.

Baiterek would benefit from developing a framework for managing impact-related risks such as just-transition or displacement risks. With a greater focus on credible impact, Baiterek's integrated risk management framework could also look at possible risks or trade-offs that the created impact might trigger. The just-transition risk would arise from Baiterek-financed investments designed to help transition the economy away from fossil fuels, which could bring an end to some jobs, make some skills unnecessary, lead to the phaseout or relocation of some industries, and harm the welfare of some population groups. The displacement risk relates to what economists call *general equilibrium effects*—and these can run across space or industries or other economic dimensions. The idea is that an investment or credit that makes one business or industry grow may take resources (labor, capital, intermediate inputs, land) from other businesses or industries, even if those are still sustainable. The resulting negative network spillovers can include shortages of workers in some industries (and a possible need for immigration of new workers) or depopulated towns with bankrupting service industries. A leading DFI needs to stay abreast of such risks and proactively manage them; the Ireland Strategic Investment Fund discussed in chapter 5 can be considered a model in this regard.

Baiterek's risk management is not fully decentralized, but a decentralized model would better suit its activities and could hedge the group against political influence. First, the scope, nature, and extent of the activities of Baiterek's subsidiaries are diverse, and the risks are usually unique and mainly limited to one legal entity. Second, the integration among Baiterek's subsidiaries is currently limited (except for the current agriculture complex—ACC and KazAgroFinance). Third, the risk management autonomy of the subsidiaries could effectively hedge them against undue political influence in their risk decisions, which is particularly relevant for the financing of large projects through DBK or bond purchases by KHC. The oversight entailed in Baiterek's risk management function covers the "three lines of defense" (3LoD) model: risk management, the internal audit function, and compliance monitoring.

The risk management, compliance monitoring, and internal audit functions should be the main integrating lines for the risk oversight function of Baiterek, complementing the decentralized risk management model. The current absence of a groupwide internal audit function calls into question the effectiveness of the 3LoD model at the group level because it may undermine Baiterek's oversight role. The internal audit function of Baiterek could be upgraded and empowered to (a) allow unrestricted access to information and all activities across the group and at each subsidiary; (b) coordinate the activities of the subsidiaries' units, in part by defining a groupwide audit plan and issuing corporate methodologies; and (c) set up relevant committees to exercise Baiterek's coordinating functions. A new compliance monitoring function, tasked with ensuring compliance with all laws, regulations, rules, and ethical codes at the groupwide level, could exert oversight and coordinate the work of the subsidiaries' compliance monitoring units. Although a shadow CRO function could be assumed by members of Baiterek's management and of subsidiaries' management, the CRO function should be explicitly established to fully satisfy the need for holistic and integrated risk management with an independent reporting line to the risk committees of the boards of directors. Holistic risk management requires covering financial, enterprise, and impact-related risks and properly consolidating all types of risks from the subsidiary to the holding level.

GOVERNANCE

To ensure proper management of impact, capital, and risk with adequate accountability, the governance structure of Baiterek Holding should be reformed, starting with the board of directors. There are three options for structuring Baiterek's Board: one that follows OECD best practice of full independence, a second one aligned with the new Samruk Kazyna model, and a third one that allows for a board with political representation—and a greater ownership function. While the former two options are preferable to ensure maximum political independence (at least on paper), political economy issues could still exist under either. There is a risk that even with these arrangements, political influence might be exerted through proxies—especially if strong civil service protections do not exist. A political board with a majority of independent professional board members and an adequate skill mix to fulfill Baiterek's double bottom line mandate is a second-best solution, but it could help consolidate the state ownership function and improve alignment with national and financial sector strategies. The ownership function is currently exercised by an MNE directorate. However, the directorate is too weak to challenge Baiterek's Board chair, the prime minister, or other political members of the board (first deputy prime minister or minister of national economy). If the first option, an independent board, is followed, then the state ownership function of the MNE directorate will need to be strengthened and possibly raised to the level of the Prime Minister's Office—also to avoid MNE's possible conflict of interest as the ministry promoting entrepreneurship. If the Samruk Kazyna model with independent members and senior civil servants is followed, the civil servant code and protections will need to be significantly strengthened. If the political model is followed, the Baiterek Board of Directors becomes the de facto state ownership unit for Baiterek and the MNE directorate a secretariat of the board. The transition to the new board model—whether political or independent—needs to be planned out to include appropriate legal actions and a nomination process and to consider business continuity needs.

Under either model, Baiterek's management, the boards of Baiterek subsidiaries, and the management of the subsidiaries must be duly isolated from political influence to ensure that medium-term impact resists the influence of political cycles. The recruitment of all board directors of the subsidiaries and the management teams of Baiterek and its subsidiaries would be based on an open international competition. The selection would be conducted by an independent private headhunting firm and vetted by an integrity due diligence firm through "fit, proper, and independence" tests. Members of the board of directors would be appointed in a staggered manner for a five-year, nonrenewable term. The management would be appointed as a team for four years. The appointment of each management team member would be renewable once, assuming successful completion of a management performance contract linked to impact KPIs. The decentralized risk management model would then keep all decisions about the activities of subsidiaries within the purview of the given subsidiary's management board. For example, DBK's large exposures would be approved by the DBK Board (the Strategic Finance Group Board shown in figure O.7) without the involvement of the board of directors of Baiterek. The clearer separation of oversight and management functions across Baiterek Holding would also require that the CEO of Baiterek not sit on the board of directors of Baiterek and that Baiterek Board members not sit on the boards of the subsidiaries.

The structure of subsidiaries appears suboptimal and could be rationalized based on the business lines' commercial, double bottom line, and fiscal agent

FIGURE O.7

Proposed reform of Baiterek's subsidiary structure

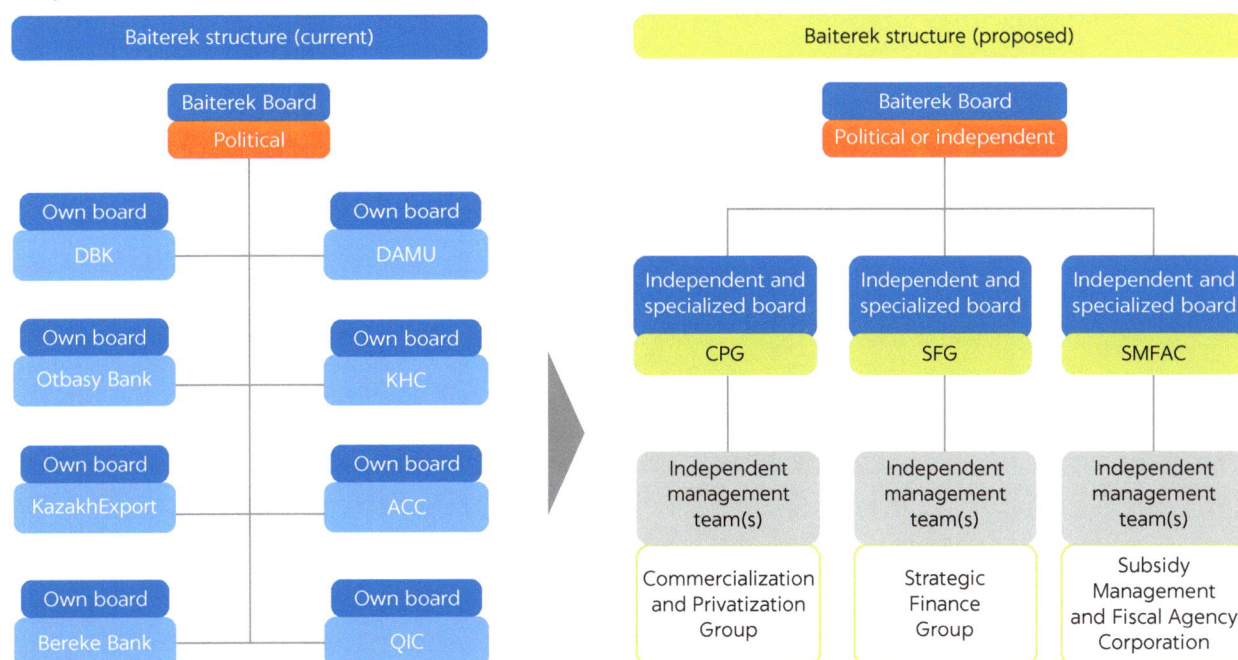

Source: World Bank.
Note: ACC = Agrarian Credit Corporation; CPG = Commercialization and Privatization Group; DAMU = Entrepreneurship Development Fund; DBK = Development Bank of Kazakhstan; KHC = Kazakhstan Housing Company; QIC = Qazaqstan Investment Corporation, JCS; SFG = Strategic Finance Group; SMFAC = Subsidy Management and Fiscal Agency Corporation.

(efficient subsidy intermediation) objectives. The current structure mixes Tier 1 and Tier 2 operations, financial market instruments and subsidies, and different areas of sectoral focus. This mixing hinders the delivery and verification of clear impact, and more importantly, limits Baiterek's ability to enhance private capital mobilization. Private capital dislikes involvement with subsidies and allocates capital depending on objectives—purely commercial and double bottom line. The new structure of Baiterek could reflect this reality in the following manner:

- *Tier 2 business lines (subsidiaries) would be grouped under the Commercialization and Privatization Group (CPG)* and the guidance of a common independent board specializing in commercialization.[10] This board could prepare most, if not all, the Tier 2 entities/business lines for eventual privatization by working with a dedicated management team or teams, depending on how consolidated the CPG corporate structure is or will become under the guidance of the CPG Board of Directors.
- *Tier 1 business lines (subsidiaries) would be grouped under the Strategic Finance Group (SFG)* and the guidance of a common independent board specializing in managing DFIs with double bottom lines (minimum financial return and maximum impact at acceptable risks).[11] This board would work with a dedicated management team or teams, depending on how consolidated the SFG corporate structure will become under the guidance of the SFG Board of Directors.
- *Provision of all subsidies would be integrated under the Subsidy Management and Fiscal Agency Corporation (SMFAC)* and the guidance of a single independent board and management team specializing in the design and implementation of subsidies. This board would aim to maximize subsidies' socioeconomic and market development impact while keeping market distortions to a minimum.

Each subsidiary group would have a common (single) board of directors exclusively composed of independent directors from the private and nongovernment sectors (figure O.7). Within each group, each subsidiary would be led by a management team exclusively composed of independent senior experts from the private and nongovernment sectors with expertise relevant to all necessary areas of business operations.

The boards overseeing the three distinct subsidiary groups require fundamentally different skills in their members to effectively fulfill the varied objectives of the groups. The CPG Board and management would comprise senior specialists from the private sector with experience in commercial and investment banking and knowledge of how to introduce new products and work existing products down the market (financial inclusion of MSMEs and households). The SFG Board and management would comprise senior experts experienced in managing DFIs with double bottom line objectives (delivery of socioeconomic and green impacts and protection of the institution's capital by achieving minimum financial returns). Both objectives would be carried out at an acceptable level of risk (financial, enterprise, and impact-related). The SMFAC Board and management would comprise senior specialists/economists with deep expertise in designing subsidies for kick-starting financial markets, niches, and products if they are missing, incomplete, or temporarily disrupted (because of systemic crises). The provision of subsidies should be temporary and avoid turning into ongoing social assistance; if needed, such assistance could be provided through other, more appropriate channels of the public sector.

Baiterek's accountability could be strengthened by improving the capacity of its enforcers and by adding new mechanisms for medium-term impact, financial soundness, and market conduct. The Parliamentary Committee on Finance and Economics often calls on Baiterek to justify its operations and impact. However, these hearings do not seem to provide worthwhile feedback that Baiterek could use and that could be reflected in operational or strategic adjustments. One reason is the alleged low capacity of the AGO, which is supposed to prepare qualified intelligence for the committee's hearings with Baiterek. The capacity of the AGO could be boosted through tailored technical assistance. This effort could be complemented by activating a new accountability mechanism focused on Baiterek's medium-term impact and enforced by AGO or ASPIR.[12] AGO or ASPIR could be responsible for commissioning (tendering and financing) periodic *independent* evaluations and making their full results openly available to the public. AGO or ASPIR would have to collaborate with and arrange for data provision from Baiterek and the Bureau of National Statistics.[13] Baiterek could also become accountable for its vast interactions with the financial market because it is a systemic financial institution (conglomerate) by any rule of thumb and competes in the market on advantageous terms.[14] The Agency for Regulation and Development of the Financial Markets (AFR) could, therefore, start supervising not only entities that take deposits (such as Otbasy) but also entities that are leaders in market segments (DAMU, ACC, KazAgroFinance) to oversee market conduct and prevent undue competitive advantage. By extension, Baiterek as a financial conglomerate could be supervised by AFR prudentially to foster financial stability and to safeguard competitive neutrality in financial markets.

The subsidy business needs to be consolidated and rationalized, and the fiscal agent function should ideally be removed from Baiterek's responsibilities and nested in the subnational fiscal framework. The subsidy intermediation business that Baiterek conducts for the government introduces governance issues through annually negotiated and uncertain funding against annually varying KPIs. The subsidy intermediation lowers the political independence of Baiterek and infringes on sound medium-term decision-making related to its core DFI business. The government should, therefore, consolidate all subsidy business in one SMFAC entity and nest the subsidy provision within the government's MTEF to provide certainty to the business line. It should negotiate funding for desired KPIs once per MTEF cycle (four to five years), together with an explicit commission fee that it will pay Baiterek for designing, implementing, and monitoring the subsidies. Baiterek is currently performing a fiscal agent function for the government—notably buying bonds of local executive authorities below market price with some netting of the pricing gap against Baiterek's obligations to the government. However, this function should not be performed by a DFI that aspires to transparently contribute to development of national financial markets and mobilization of private capital. This fiscal agent function should be isolated from Baiterek's core DFI business and nested within the subnational fiscal and debt management framework.

A complete list of technical recommendations and policy options is provided in appendix A; table O.1 lists main (priority) recommendations. The government may wish to adopt the recommendations in their entirety or to select only some based on political feasibility. After selected recommendations are

TABLE O.1 Main (priority) recommendations

RECOMMENDATION	RESPONSIBLE ENTITY
1. Clarify Baiterek's mandate and policy role in relation to the national and financial sector strategies and across its development finance, commercial, and fiscal agent objectives/functions.	GoK
2. Enhance the focus on Baiterek's delivery of impact and economic additionality for both the end-beneficiaries and the development of financial markets, adding a green impact dimension.	MNE, GoK
3. Reform the subsidiary structure so Baiterek can better support financial market creation and private capital mobilization, isolate subsidy intermediation, and wind down fiscal agent functions.	MNE, Baiterek Holding
4. Reconsider the model for Baiterek's Board of Directors and ensure the independence of management teams and boards of subsidiaries. Clearly separate the oversight functions from management functions throughout Baiterek Holding.	MNE, GoK
5. Strengthen risk management through full decentralization, upgrade internal audit and compliance to group-level functions, and safeguard underwriting of credit risk at the DBK level from political influence.	Baiterek
6. Improve project and program selection decisions by selecting large projects and programs based on the maximized economic rate of return subject to a minimum internal rate of return (hurdle rate) and by developing a robust flagging system for small projects under support programs.	Baiterek
7. Extend the regulatory and supervisory framework to Baiterek on a consolidated basis, refrain from excluding Otbasy from AFR's regulation and supervision, and consider including DBK and ACC (and KHC) on a solo basis.	MNE, MoF, AFR
8. Boost the accountability mechanism via the Parliamentary Committee on Finance and Economics, annually evaluate impacts reported by specialized companies, and periodically conduct impact evaluation commissioned by AGO or ASPIR.	MNE, GoK
9. Enhance disclosures of beneficiary-level data and PFI-level data to enable assessments by think tanks and researchers and to improve fiscal reporting of Baiterek funding and fiscal contingent liabilities.	Baiterek, MNE, MoF

Source: World Bank.
Note: ACC = Agrarian Credit Corporation; AFR = Agency for Regulation and Development of the Financial Markets; AGO = Auditor General Office; ASPIR = Agency for Strategic Planning and Reforms; DBK = Development Bank of Kazakhstan; GoK = government of Kazakhstan; KHC = Kazakhstan Housing Company; MNE = Ministry of National Economy; MoF = Ministry of Finance; PFI = participating financial institution.

endorsed and preferred policy options decided upon, the government could develop a detailed roadmap of implementation actions that are properly sequenced, with assigned functional responsibility and timelines for implementation. The roadmap could encompass actions that tackle the reform agenda through both the top-down and bottom-up approaches. Top-down approaches—such as policy reforms and legal and regulatory actions—are comprehensive, but they take longer to implement and are slower to effect change, including in the corporate culture. Therefore, complementary bottom-up actions are often used in change management to launch pilots that can have demonstrative effects and change corporate culture from within. Such pilots help create centers of excellence—professional drivers of change that generate positive spillovers throughout the organization. The pilots could involve the development of innovative projects that leverage knowledge exchange and technical assistance from role model peers or multilateral development banks. They could also focus on product innovation and entry into new market niches that have well-identified market imperfections or involve large asymmetric information or coordination failures—such as private catastrophe insurance and other sustainable finance provision, equity risk guarantee and hedging (derivatives) market development, factoring services, or digital finance platforms, among others.

NOTES

1. Kazyna Capital Management (KCM) was rebranded as QIC in 2023.
2. The LEA bonds purchased by Baiterek (Kazakhstan Housing Company [KHC]) amounted to T 163.7 billion (2021) and T 281.2 billion (2020). Invested assets amounted to T 1,785 billion. However, if the calculation excludes foreign government securities, National Bank of Kazakhstan bonds, government bonds, purchased or originated credit-impaired assets, and similar items, then the remaining balance is T 63 billion (mostly corporate bonds and shares). Subsidies received amounted to T 326 billion (2021), but net of asset-side and other adjustments, the figure is reduced to T 161.5 billion.
3. The board of directors includes the first deputy prime minister; the deputy chief of staff of the Presidential Administration; the ministers of finance, national economy, industry, and infrastructure development; the CEO of Baiterek; and three independent directors who chair the strategic, audit, and remuneration committees.
4. Enterprise risks may be operational or related to anti–money laundering/combating the financing of terrorism (AML/CFT), business continuity, or environmental footprint.
5. The 2030 financial sector development concept was approved in September 2022.
6. Social housing programs should be implemented by other government agencies.
7. Gradually, the calculations for carbon emissions should advance from using GHG Protocol Scope 2 to Scope 3 for the invested or financed projects/activities. The World Bank methodology for shadow price calculation should serve as a starting reference.
8. Adding KPIs to increase the sum of ERRs to justify project selection should be prohibited within the period for which the impact framework is set.
9. See, for example, Melecky (2021) and references therein.
10. Because legally each joint stock company (JSC) has to have its board, the board members would sit on all the boards of the JSCs within CPG. The board meetings would then be held jointly or consecutively for all entities within the group. The board would also provide guidance and decisions on useful mergers within the group.
11. Because legally each JSC has to have its board, the board members would sit on all boards of the JSCs within SFG. The board meetings would be then held jointly or consecutively for all entities within the group. The board would also provide guidance and decisions on useful mergers within the group.
12. One mandate of ASPIR is assessing the impact of longer-term reforms.
13. The collaboration would help ensure proper identification, including data on treatments, counterfactuals, and confounding factors.
14. It leads the activity in several market segments (mortgage lending, MSME lending, agricultural lending) while benefiting from the implicit state guarantee.

REFERENCES

Bova, M. E., M. Ruiz-Arranz, M. F. G. Toscani, and H. E. Ture. 2016. "The Fiscal Costs of Contingent Liabilities: A New Dataset." IMF Working Paper 16/14, International Monetary Fund, Washington, DC.

Böwer, U. 2017. "State-Owned Enterprises in Emerging Europe: The Good, the Bad, and the Ugly." IMF Working Paper 17/221, International Monetary Fund, Washington, DC.

Eliasson, J., and M. Lundberg. 2012. "Do Cost-Benefit Analyses Influence Transport Investment Decisions? Experiences from the Swedish Transport Investment Plan 2010–21." *Transport Reviews* 32 (1): 29–48.

Florio, M., V. Morretta, and W. Willak. 2018. "Cost-Benefit Analysis and European Union Cohesion Policy: Economic versus Financial Returns in Investment Project Appraisal." *Journal of Benefit-Cost Analysis* 9 (1): 147–80.

Levy-Yeyati, E. L., A. Micco, and U. Panizza. 2004. "Should the Government Be in the Banking Business? The Role of State-Owned and Development Banks." Working Paper 517, Inter-American Development Bank, Research Department.

Melecky, M. 2021. *Hidden Debt: Solutions to Avert the Next Financial Crisis in South Asia*. South Asia Development Matters. Washington, DC: World Bank. https://openknowledge.worldbank.org/handle/10986/35595.

Mishan, E. J., and E. Quah. 2020. *Cost-Benefit Analysis*. New York: Routledge.

1 Stylized Facts and Trends for Baiterek

INTRODUCTION

On May 22, 2013, the president of Kazakhstan established Baiterek National Management Holding, a joint stock company (JSC) intended to develop the national economy by streamlining the operations of development finance institutions (DFIs) with state participation. Baiterek Holding's structure, including the missions and business lines of its subsidiaries, is summarized in figure 1.1. Baiterek's total consolidated assets grew from 5.6 percent of gross domestic product (GDP) in 2013, the year it was established, to about 12 percent in 2021 (figure 1.2)[1]. In recent years, the growth of assets has been fueled mainly by the issuance of debt securities and funds attracted from clients (figure 1.3). After reaching a peak number of 11 subsidiaries in 2014, Baiterek consolidated its subsidiary structure to seven subsidiaries in October 2022. The number of subsidiaries grew again to eight with the takeover (nationalization) of Sberbank's subsidiary due to the exit of the Russian state-owned Sberbank from Kazakhstan. Baiterek Holding plays a dual role as a DFI and a fiscal agent—notably by intermediating state budget funds for financial service subsidies and buying/financing bonds of subnational entities.

Private sector development is one of Baiterek's key priorities. Its subsidiaries perform a key role in facilitating private sector development. In 2013, Baiterek assumed the ownership and management of DAMU (the Entrepreneurship Development Fund) to support the sustainable development of micro, small, and medium enterprises (MSMEs). Conditional placement of funds, interest rate subsidies, and partial loan guarantees are the three major instruments used by DAMU to support MSMEs. The interest rate subsidies often receive government support, and in 2021 they amounted to more than T 122 billion. Also in 2013, Baiterek assumed the ownership and management of Kazyna Capital Management (KCM) JSC as the legal entity responsible for developing the private equity/venture capital ecosystem. Baiterek Venture Fund invests in companies operating in high-priority sectors, while the Leaders of Competitiveness–National Champions Program supports companies that intend to establish their niche in the Eurasian Economic Union. In 2018, the board of directors of Baiterek amended its private sector investment policy to prioritize sustainable socioeconomic development. In 2019, the National Agency for Technological

FIGURE 1.1

Structure of Baiterek Holding with subsidiaries' missions and business lines

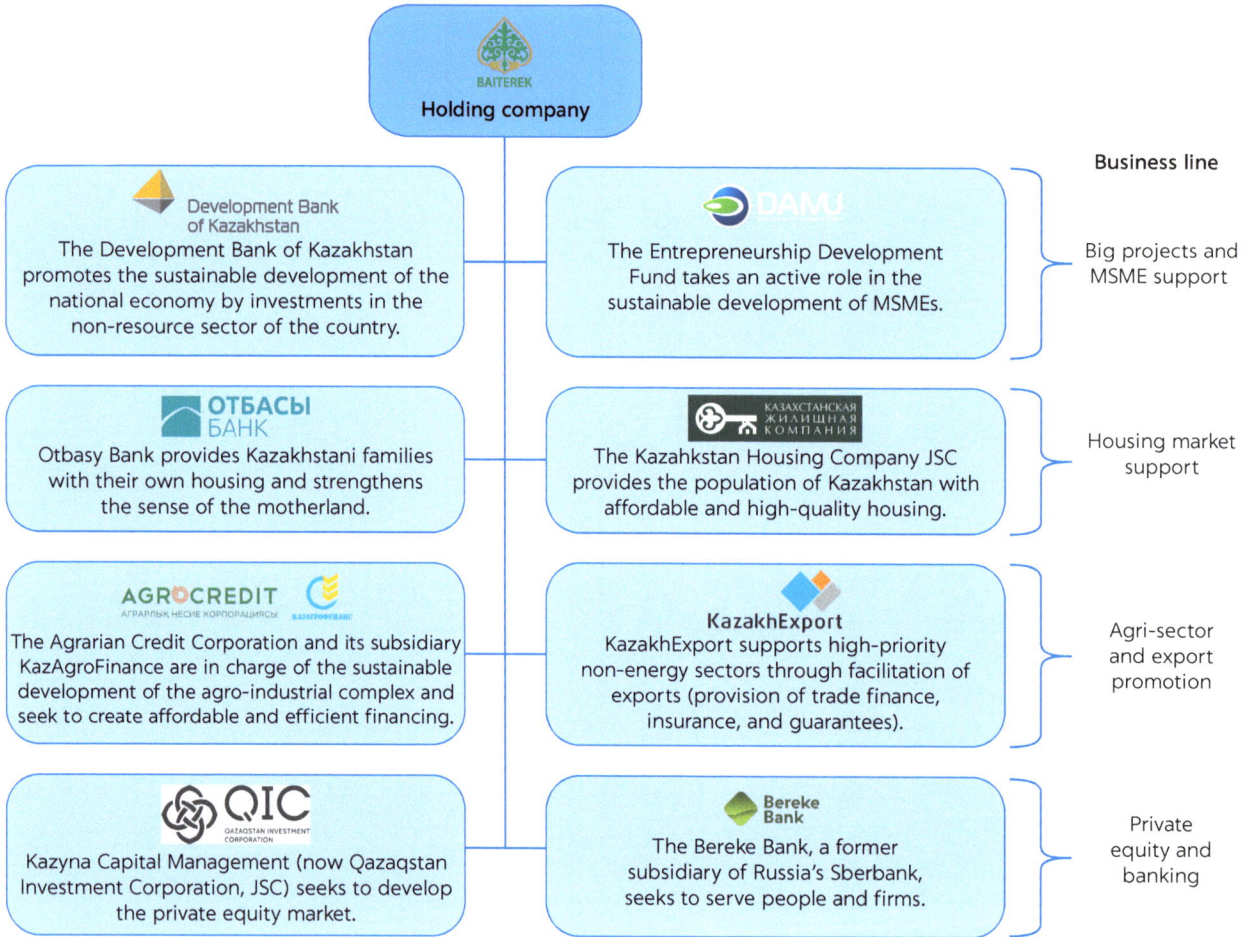

Source: World Bank based on Baiterek's website, https://baiterek.gov.kz/en/.
Note: MSME = micro, small, and medium enterprises.

FIGURE 1.2

Baiterek's total assets and share in the economy

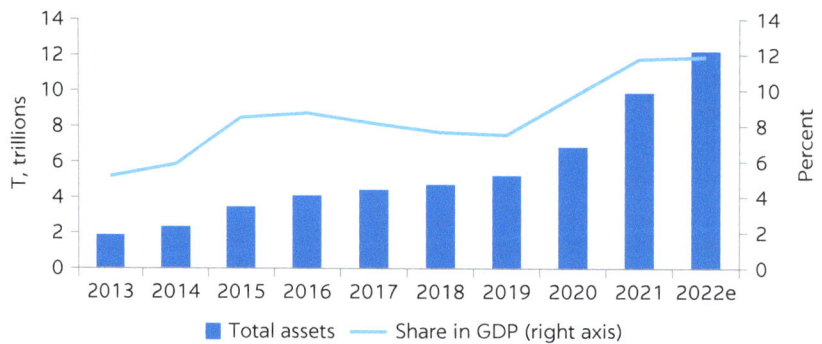

Sources: Baiterek National Management Holding JSC; Committee of Statistics.
Note: 2022 numbers are estimated. GDP = gross domestic product.

FIGURE 1.3

Dynamics and composition of Baiterek's total liabilities

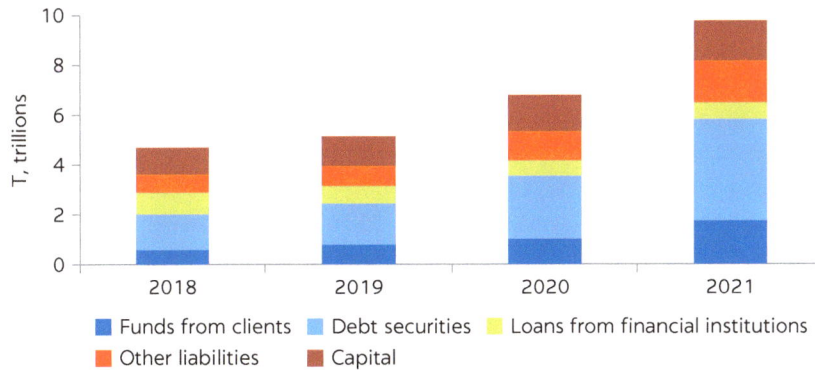

Source: Baiterek National Management Holding JSC.
Note: Funds from clients mainly comprise deposits of Otbasy Bank.

Development JSC was transformed into QazTech Ventures JSC to support venture capital market development, business incubation, and new technology adoption by entrepreneurs. In June 2022, QazTech Ventures merged into Qazaqstan Investment Corporation (QIC) as part of Baiterek's reorganization to streamline operations along major business lines.[2]

Infrastructure development is one of Baiterek's core operations. In 2014, Baiterek started to play an active role in national infrastructure development, mainly through the Development Bank of Kazakhstan (DBK), whose primary mission is to promote the sustainable development of the national economy by investing in the non-resource sector. In 2014, DBK become the operator of Nurly Zhol, a state infrastructure development program mainly funded by the government budget.[3] Baiterek was also involved in establishing the PPP [Public-Private Partnership] Projects Support Center LLP, which facilitated private sector involvement in developing the country's infrastructure. In 2016, this institution was renamed the Kazakhstan Project Preparation Fund LLP and its mandate was expanded. By 2022, however, the institution had been wound down.

Baiterek is Kazakhstan's key actor in housing market development. Baiterek started its contributions to the development of the housing market through the Regional Development Program and the Housing Construction Guarantee Fund (HCGF). In 2017, Baiterek became a single operator of the Nurly Zher, a widely used state housing construction program that encourages saving beginning in childhood to enable access to affordable mortgages in adulthood. The optimization of Baiterek's housing operations continued during the COVID-19 pandemic, when operations of Baiterek Development JSC and HCGF were merged into the Kazakhstan Mortgage Company JSC, which guarantees and subsidizes housing development projects and construction as a wholesale institution.[4] Otbasy Bank, another subsidiary of Baiterek Holding, is now in charge of retail housing loans and mortgage lending, accounting for nearly 66 percent of all mortgage loans in the country. As of 2022, Otbasy Bank and the Kazakhstan Housing Company (KHC)—both Baiterek subsidiaries—were the sole operators of the Nurly Zher program.

Baiterek's support of export-oriented companies contributes to the diversification of the economy. For example, Export Insurance Company KazakhExport JSC (KazakhExport) was established to promote exports of non-mining goods and services. The main instruments of KazakhExport include trade finance and insurance; as of 2021, total notional amounts of these instruments reached T 326.5 billion and T 204.7 billion, respectively.

In 2021, Baiterek took on the mandate for promoting agricultural financing through its integration with KazAgro Holding. The Agrarian Credit Corporation (ACC) JSC and KazAgroFinance JSC (KazAgro) became Baiterek subsidiaries after their former parent company KazAgro Holding was merged into Baiterek.[5] The two subsidiaries are responsible for developing the agro-industrial complex through industrialization and diversification based on sustainable and affordable financing schemes. In 2022, further restructuring resulted in KazAgroFinance becoming a direct subsidiary of ACC.

By August 2022, Baiterek's holding structure included eight subsidiary entities. These have mandates in small and medium enterprise (SME) lending and private equity/venture capital market development, access to housing finance, agricultural financing, export financing, large projects, and infrastructure financing. Figure 1.4 depicts the share of the subsidiaries' assets in the total assets of the holding company. Among the subsidiaries, there is a mix of Tier 1 entities (that operate wholesale) and Tier 2 entities (that directly compete with private commercial institutions). For example, ACC provides funding to banks and microfinance institutions for agricultural loans but also lends directly to agricultural businesses. QIC (formerly KCM) operates as a fund of funds but also manages captive funds. The Otbasy Bank is a fully fledged commercial (deposit-taking) Tier 2 bank, while KHC operates as a Tier 1 (wholesale level) bank. Preferred loans and subsidies from the state still play an important role in the growth of Baiterek subsidiaries, but their share in total liabilities is gradually decreasing (figure 1.5).

In parallel, Baiterek took important steps to improve its vision, governance, and organization in 2017. These steps included approving the Development

FIGURE 1.4

Subsidiaries' assets as a percentage of total assets of Baiterek, 2021

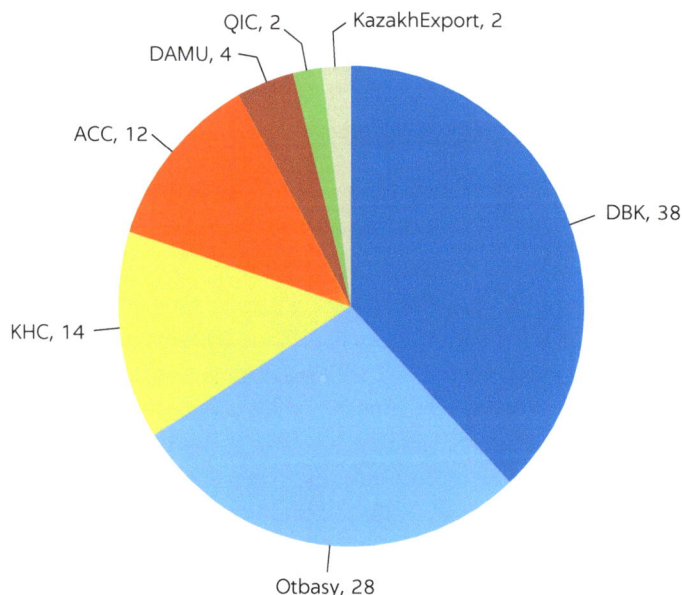

Source: Baiterek National Management Holding JSC.
Note: Bereke (Sberbank) is not shown due to consolidation issues. ACC = Agrarian Credit Corporation; DAMU = Entrepreneurship Development Fund; DBK = Development Bank of Kazakhstan; KHC = Kazakhstan Housing Company; QIC = Qazaqstan Investment Corporation, JSC.

FIGURE 1.5

Government support to Baiterek (loans and subsidies)

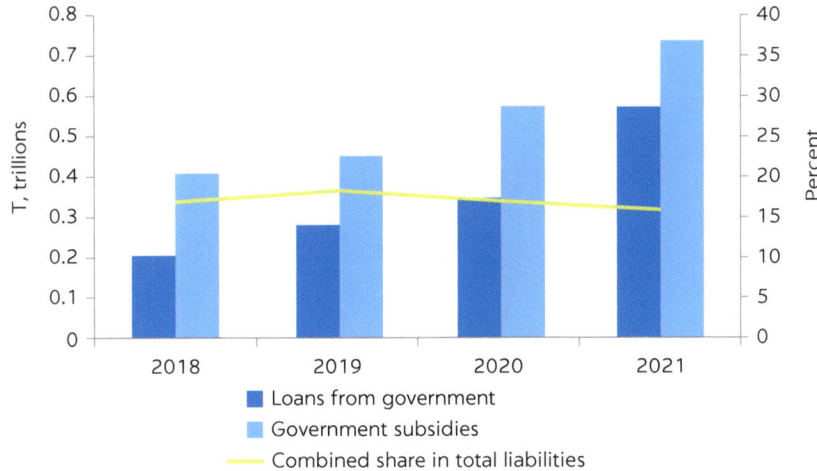

Source: Baiterek National Management Holding JSC.
Note: Numbers stand for the remaining balances at the end of the period.

FIGURE 1.6

Composition of Baiterek's consolidated assets

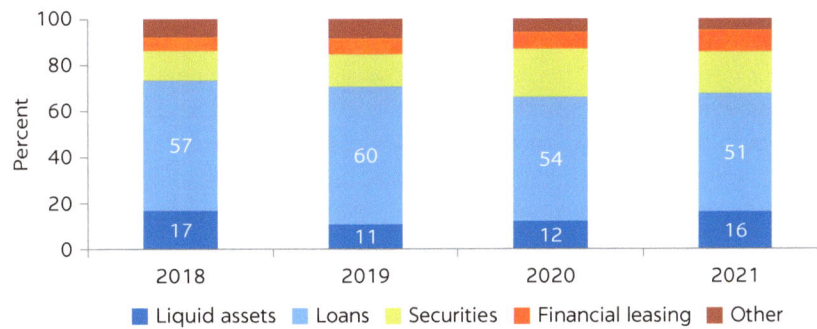

Source: Baiterek National Management Holding JSC.
Note: Bereke (Sberbank) is not included due to consolidation issues.

Strategy until 2023 and renewing its Code for Corporate Governance. In 2017, Baiterek also improved the digitization of its operations by establishing a single portal for entrepreneurship support. This portal digitized the processes for application submission and status tracking, and made it possible to maintain a unified database of clients, with detailed information on companies' background, projects, and business interactions.

Asset and loan portfolio compositions have changed substantially in recent years. COVID-19 had a negative impact on Baiterek's lending activity. Between 2019 and 2021, the share of loans in total assets decreased from 60 percent to 51 percent, and the share of liquid assets jumped from 11 percent to 16 percent (figure 1.6). In recent years, mortgage and construction loans have been increasing rapidly and, in 2022, they represented more than half of the loan portfolio (figure 1.7). Concentration risk is relatively high because more than 90 percent of loans are concentrated in four sectors.

FIGURE 1.7
Composition of Baiterek's loan portfolio (loans and financial leasing), 2021
percent

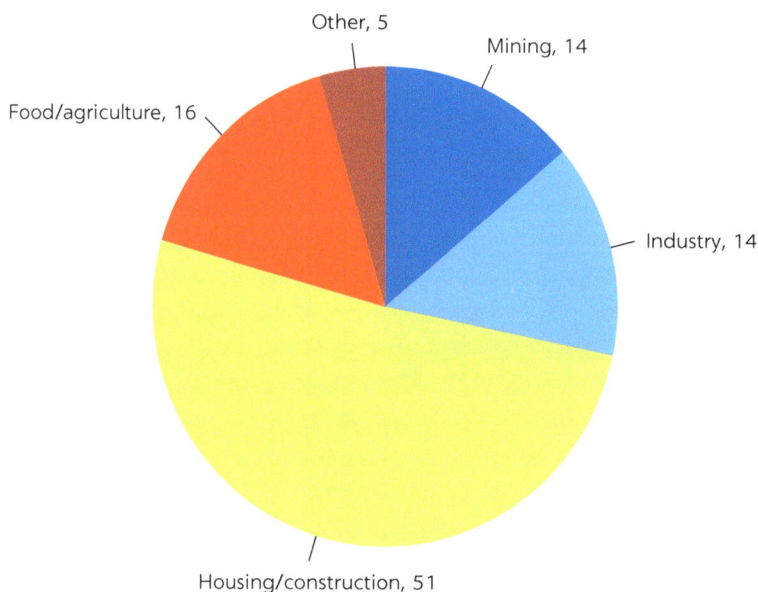

Sources: Baiterek National Management Holding JSC; World Bank staff estimates.
Note: The reported numbers cover only major lenders (Development Bank of Kazakhstan, Agrarian Credit Corporation, Otbasy Bank, and Kazakhstan Housing Company).

Debt instruments are becoming an important source for funding Baiterek's operations, in line with the strategic objective of raising more funds from private sources. In 2018, Baiterek issued T 77.7 billion in 15-year bonds on the Kazakhstan Stock Exchange (KASE). In 2019, it continued tapping domestic capital markets by offering two bond issues worth T 40 and T 25 billion, respectively. In 2020, during the turbulent COVID-19 period, Baiterek placed bonds worth T 150 billion on KASE. In 2021, Baiterek again tapped local capital markets through the issuance of T 50 billion in 10-year bonds.

SUMMARY OF RECENT ACTIVITY

Baiterek's size has been increasing at a rapid pace. In 2021, its total assets increased by 45 percent and reached about T 10 trillion (roughly $23.2 billion, or 11 percent of Kazakhstan's GDP). The increase in total assets was mainly funded by the growth in debt liabilities equal to T 2.8 trillion. As a result, the leverage ratio of the holding company rose substantially, from 3.8 in 2020 to 4.9 in 2021.

On the surface, Baiterek's capitalization, profitability, and liquidity do not raise major concerns; however, material financial risks may not be properly consolidated. In 2021, after acquiring KazAgro Holding, Baiterek reported a consolidated leverage (debt to capital) ratio of 4.9. The return on assets (ROA) and return on equity (ROE) stood at 1.3 percent and 7.2 percent, respectively, in 2021. ROE diverged significantly across Baiterek's subsidiaries, ranging from 1.0 percent to 19.8 percent; the worst performer was QIC and the best was Otbasy Bank. Liquidity risk is mitigated by government guarantees, low leverage, the increasing diversification of funding sources, and centralized management of intragroup liquidity flows. Liquid assets in the form of cash and equivalents increased 2.5 times between 2020 and 2021, representing close to 17 percent of total liabilities. Similarly, past losses have triggered a more conservative risk appetite for interbank lending and foreign exchange open positions. Baiterek and its subsidiaries—notably DBK—were able to issue bonds in tenge, US dollars, and rubles, which could expose them to some market and exchange rate risk. See appendix B for an overview of key available financials.

Financial support to SMEs is expanding. Loans to SMEs showed a substantial increase, from T 1.7 trillion in 2020 to T 2.2 trillion in 2021. SME loans granted by Baiterek—notably through its subsidiary DAMU—represented 2.7 percent of GDP in 2021 and about 40 percent of all SME credit. Total SME lending in Kazakhstan stood at 6.7 percent of GDP, which reflects significant room for growth. Baiterek carries a great responsibility for creating a deeper and healthier SME lending market—one that, following the Baiterek financial support programs, can scale up the delivery of green and other beneficial socioeconomic impacts. Financial support to SMEs is provided mainly through DAMU in the form of conditional placement funds (CPFs), subsidized interest rates (SIRs), and partial loan guarantees (PLGs). In 2021, the number of participants in CPFs decreased by 30 percent to 7,783 enterprises. However, the number of participants in the other two programs increased substantially: SIRs rose by 17,672 to 32,351 participants, and PLGs rose by 9,873 to 17,219 participants. As a result, SIRs, the most market-distortionary instrument among the three, now represent more than 73 percent of the financing support provided to SMEs.

Baiterek is utilizing both supply- and demand-side mechanisms to develop the housing market. In 2021, supply-side support provided by KHC reached T 598.4 billion, including guarantees, bond purchases, and other financial instruments. The demand-side support by KHC totaled T 81.1 billion; it included acquiring the rights of claim on mortgage loans, issuing mortgage loans under the Orda Program (a subsidized mortgage program phased out in October 2021), and providing housing under the rent-with-purchase program. In 2021, the Otbasy Bank increased its mortgage loan portfolio by 100 percent to reach a total of T 1,235 billion. As a result, Otbasy Bank's share in the mortgage lending market increased by 800 basis points to 66 percent—a situation that may not support crowding in of other second-tier banks. Otbasy also accepts deposits linked to housing construction. The number of depositors increased by 601,370 individuals in 2021, bringing total depositors as a share of Kazakhstan's economically active population to 24 percent.

REPORTED AND PERCEIVED IMPACT

On its website, Baiterek reports sizable development impact on job creation and growth of businesses, but issues of attribution and double or triple counting cast doubt about impact measurement (figure 1.8). In 2021, Baiterek reported that it created 9,420 jobs, contributed to production of manufacturing sector output of T 13.5 trillion, and facilitated the export of goods worth T 2.6 trillion. Also in 2021, the tax payments of Baiterek's beneficiaries reached T 1.7 trillion. However, any beneficiary firm reports the growth of jobs and output by attributing all of them to Baiterek's support. Moreover, if a business benefits from two (or three) support mechanisms (interest subsidy, credit guarantee), the impact on jobs and output gets double- (or triple-) counted. There is simply no effort to consider

FIGURE 1.8

Impact of subsidiaries on specific sectors and job creation

Development Bank of Kazakhstan
- In 2021, invested T 399.1 billion in manufacturing and T 134.1 billion in infrastructure sectors
- Provided T 168.4 billion in loans to support exports
- Financed 37 major projects, including construction of 50 MW solar power plant in Kostanay region
- These projects created 1,876 new permanent jobs

Entrepreneurship Development Fund
- In 2021, provided interest subsidies to more than 32,000 projects and partial guarantees to more than 17,000 projects
- Saved 797,000 jobs and created 217,000 new jobs since establishment
- Provided T 9.2 trillion in financial support to more than 156,000 projects since establishment
- Companies receiving financial support paid T 4.0 trillion in taxes

Otbasy Bank
- In 2021, provided housing to 82,252 families using its own funds and to 20,290 families under the Nurly Zher program
- Currently has 2,196,865 depositers owning T 1.5 trillion
- Of these, 1 in 10 is a child deposit

Kazakhstan Housing Company
- In 2021, supply-side programs provided housing to 30,047 families
- Demand-side programs provided housing to 2,503 families
- Purchased T 751.7 billion in local executive authority bonds, which supported 6,743 projects employing more than 250,000

Agrarian Credit Corporation
- In 2021, provided T 322.5 billion in financing to more than 20,000 agricultural producers
- Issued 11,100 microcredits worth T 68.6 to develop entrepreneurship
- Holds 163 insurance contracts with premium subsidies totaling T 242.6 million and payouts of T 825.3 milllion
- ACC's operations created more than 9,000 jobs between 2017 and 2021

KazakhExport
- In 2021, supported 81 exporters, including 26 new customers
- These companies generated export revenue of T 213.8 billion
- Value of export contracts reached T 326.5 billion
- Assumed insurance obligation worth T 204.7 billion

Kazyna Capital Management (now Qazaqstan Investment Corporation, JSC)
- In 2021, new investments reached T 36.7 billion: T 12 billion for transport infrastructure, T 12.8 billion for agro-industrial complex; T 404 million for media and entertainment, T 1.5 billion for information technology, and T 8.5 billion for other
- In 2021, 895 new jobs were created

Source: Baiterek website, https://baiterek.gov.kz/en/.

counterfactuals (growth of similar businesses that did not receive support) or isolate (or at least prorate) the differential impacts of individual support mechanisms.

Stakeholders and market participants have expressed concerns about the market creation impact of Baiterek and its subsidiaries. The Association of Financiers has indirectly expressed concerns about the distortionary effect of interest subsidies on the efficiency of credit allocation as well as MSMEs' access to finance, and has called for shifting state support to more market-based programs (Interfax Kazakhstan 2021). The rapid growth of mortgage loans extended by Otbasy makes it the single most dominant player driving this market; private commercial lenders are falling behind over concerns of being crowded out from the mortgage market, which they should drive in the long term (Sarsenova 2021). Moreover, the government decision to exempt the Otbasy Bank from the prudential supervision of the Agency for Regulation and Development of the

Financial Markets lacks a clear rationale. The decision also risks creating an uneven playing field by allowing expansion of the quasi-fiscal sector at the expense of the private sector. Such expansion would negatively affect the scope of financial intermediation and the pace of market development in the medium and long run. The ACC and KazAgroFinance dominate lending and leasing to the agriculture sector without a clear strategy for crowding private capital into this lending segment. Concerns about the integrity of DBK lending have culminated in the president's critique and call for reform (*Tengri News* 2022). While the government and Baiterek chose to intervene with support measures in some financial service markets, they seem to leave out others, such as insurance (apart from agricultural and export insurance) or digital payment services.

NOTES

1. Unless otherwise indicated, statistics on Baiterek presented in this study draw on annual reports of Baiterek and its subsidiaries.
2. KCM had formerly been rebranded as the Qazaqstan Investment Corporation (QIC).
3. DBK is an operator of several government programs, including the Nurly Zhol Infrastructure Development Program for 2015–2019, the lending program for large-scale businesses in the manufacturing sector, the State Program for Industrial and Innovative Development for 2015–2019, the State Program for Industrial and Innovative Development for 2020–2025, and the Business Road Map 2025 program. The effectiveness of some of these programs was challenged when President Tokayev criticized DBK's activities after the January 2022 unrest. See *Tengri News* (2022).
4. Baiterek Development JSC—since liquidated—stimulated supply in the housing market through the financing of construction.
5. KazAgro was established by the government of Kazakhstan in 1999 to deal with the major challenge faced by the agricultural sector: renovation of outdated machinery and technology. KazAgro's main operation was financial leasing. In 2022, KazAgro was merged into ACC, a subsidiary of Baiterek, to streamline government support to the agricultural sector.

REFERENCES

Interfax Kazakhstan. 2021. "Chairperson of the Management Board of the Association of Financiers of Kazakhstan Elena Bakhmutova: In the Case of Continuation of State Support for Ineffective Companies, the Risk of Zombie Business Emergence Is Real" [in Russian]. June 2021. https://www.interfax.kz/?lang=eng&int_id=13&news_id=232.

Sarsenova, Meruert. 2021. "What Will Contribute to the Emergence of New Mortgage Products" [in Russian]. Association of Financiers of Kazakhstan. September 5, 2021. https://afk.kz/ru/publikaczii-v-smi/intervyu/chto-budet-sposobstvovat-poyavleniyu-novyix-ipotechnyix-produktov.html.

Tengri News. 2022. "Development Bank of Kazakhstan Has Become a Personal Bank for the Elite—Tokayev" [in Russian]. January 11, 2022. https://tengrinews.kz/kazakhstan_news/bank-razvitiya-kazahstana-prevratilsya-lichnyiy-bank-458777/.

2 Baiterek as a Policy Tool

Kazakhstan needs to spur the participation of the private financial sector in financing economic activity, and Baiterek Holding has been the country's primary direct policy tool for this purpose. With the banking sector credit-to-GDP (gross domestic product) ratio still at a shallow 25 percent, Kazakhstan falls markedly behind its regional peers. Despite multiple government support programs, private sector credit to the real economy has contracted in real terms in the recent past due to banking and corporate sector weaknesses. The main driver of recent credit growth has been consumer and mortgage lending—the latter mostly fueled by state support programs.[1] Baiterek, through its subsidiaries, is the key administrator of the government financial support programs and the conglomerate of development finance institutions whose on–balance sheet resources amount to more than 12 percent of GDP—excluding other significant budget resources flowing through Baiterek on the basis of its fiscal agent role (growth rate of assets averaged 23 percent during the last five years).

In 2022, the government of Kazakhstan approved a strategy to strengthen the role of financial services as an instrumental driver of economic growth. The Agency for Regulation and Development of the Financial Markets (AFR), in conjunction with key stakeholders such as the National Bank of Kazakhstan (NBK), the Ministry of National Economy (MNE), and various financial service associations, has drafted the Concept for the Development of the Financial Sector of Kazakhstan 2030. The concept relies on five pillars and suggests focusing on financial stability and sustainability while tapping the immense potential of new technologies to increase the efficiency and reach of financial services. Overall, the concept aims to develop competition, create equal operating conditions for all financial institutions, and increase financial inclusion and equitable access to financial products and services for all firms and consumers.

State dominance in the financial systems remains another critical issue to address. While all its measures are ultimately designed to better integrate Kazakhstan's financial services into the international arena and improve the welfare of the population, the concept document suggests decreasing the significant share of state participation in direct lending to the economy and in market-distorting business and consumer subsidies. In addition, the government plans to gradually reduce state financial support focused on direct financing of the economy; thanks to indirect government support (risk sharing), this step should ensure that financial market resources replace state financing in large, capital-intensive investment projects.

The 2050 National Development Strategy sets a new course of reforms grounded in economic and social modernization. Following the first strategy, adopted in 1997, and the mid-term strategy 2025, the 2050 strategy is currently the key national strategy document. Together with the 2030 concept strategy related to the financial sector and the 2030 strategy related to public administration reform, the 2050 strategy sets the course of action for Baiterek and identifies seven priorities.[2] Creating a favorable investment climate, promoting an effective public-private partnership, and adopting modern corporate governance practices for the state are at the core of the transformation path and will require rethinking the state's role. Baiterek sits at the center of this course of reform as an instrumental financier of the private sector, a key player in building partnerships with the private sector, and a potential champion of corporate governance, including in sustainable finance.

The bundle of national and sectoral policies coupled with the agreed strategic thematic priorities defines the scope of Baiterek as a policy tool. Sustainable growth, support for agribusiness, fostering of entrepreneurship, and strengthening of regions are some the key thematic priorities that define the strategic directions for Baiterek Holding and its subsidiaries.

Targets and key performance indicators (KPIs) are set according to these priorities, but the process appears cumbersome. The MNE outsources macroanalysis and target estimates to a dedicated think tank (Institute of National Economics). The think tank circulates the analysis and estimates among various line ministries, which return targets and KPIs to MNE. MNE then communicates targets and KPIs via a letter of expectations to Baiterek. This initial letter bundles around 30 KPIs, which are then consolidated by Baiterek into 10–12 KPIs (the new strategy will have only nine). Bringing down the number of KPIs requires negotiations with the respective line ministries that last on average at least six months. Once agreement is achieved, KPIs are communicated to the office of the Presidential Administration, cleared, and then returned to the Baiterek Board for final ratification. Once back at the board, the KPIs are recirculated among the respective departmental line ministries for another round of feedback before approval by the board. Interviews have revealed that the process is complex and too lengthy, opening the door to political influence over Baiterek's development goals in the short term and across the political cycle. In 2019, this process started in November and ended two years later. Ultimately, the process appears duplicative because the ministers sitting on the Baiterek Board head the same ministries that propose sectoral targets.

Developing adequate KPIs and KPI targets remains critical for Baiterek's ability to assess the performance of the holding company at both the aggregate level and the subsidiary level. Further discussions with several stakeholders involved in the process have confirmed the complexity of aggregating what each entity at Baiterek contributes, and in what capacity. But once contributions are aggregated, identifying what share each subsidiary has contributed to the targets is likewise complex; as a result, performance monitoring against the target of each single subsidiary is difficult. Performance monitoring can be especially difficult in several sectors where Baiterek may have a role in both the demand and supply sides, and where KPIs may be designed to capture both sides. In the housing market, for example, KPIs may blur attempts to aggregate the contribution to the supply of more affordable housing and the contribution to the provision of financing for purchases of affordable housing.

Enhancing the ability to quantify the green impact of operations and assess performance should be priorities for Baiterek and MNE moving forward. The purpose of Baiterek remains strongly anchored in developmental goals, such as promoting sustainable economic development for the country and promoting economic diversification. In this respect, targets and KPIs could be better weighted and integrated with calculations of carbon emissions and the social cost of carbon, and the Baiterek mission statement could integrate environmental, social, and governance (ESG) considerations and reflect an ESG strategy and contributions to the country's Nationally Determined Contribution. The Irish International Sustainable Finance Centre (box 2.1) presents several options for performance monitoring that Baiterek could consider. Quarterly reporting could speed up agreement on KPIs and targets, the impact assessment could keep operations more focused on social objectives, and the baseline assessment could prove very useful in keeping track of international commitments. The methodological approach to sustainable finance becomes critical to track progress on all fronts, and Baiterek should finalize a methodology to this end.

Baiterek's mission statement could be advanced considering new country (and global) priorities and (as indicated previously) could include ESG

BOX 2.1

Impact and performance assessment: The case of the Irish International Sustainable Finance Centre

The Irish government established the International Sustainable Finance Centre of Excellence as one of 18 actions identified in the Sustainable Finance Roadmap issued in 2021. The center will partner with the Financial Centres for Sustainability (FC4S) network, which is hosted by the United Nations Development Programme. It will focus on accelerating the sustainable finance agenda at policy, regulatory, and market levels, and will carry out research and development activities aimed at supporting the design, development, and launch of innovative financial mechanisms to facilitate the transition to a sustainable economy.

The center has decided to assess its impact via three measures:

1. *Annual progress report and impact assessment.* On a quarterly basis, progress is reported using a traffic-light system. These quarterly reports form the basis of an annual progress report. An impact assessment is conducted to determine progress toward the Irish commitment to the United Nations Sustainable Development Goals

(SDGs) and net neutrality from the financial market's perspective. The assessment investigates Ireland's financing gap and the impact of sustainable finance on the real economy, including the extent to which it supports delivery of the National Climate Action Plans and the SDGs.

2. *Annual baseline assessment.* The annual baseline assessment uses the FC4S methodology and the Sustainable Finance Observatory platform to track and measure on a quarterly basis Irish progress against internationally recognized commitments, such as those under the Task Force on Climate-Related Financial Disclosures, net zero carbon emissions, and science-based targets.

3. *Ireland for Finance annual strategy and action plan development.* During the fourth quarter of every year, the Department of Finance engages with all stakeholders as they develop the following year's action plan. On an ongoing quarterly basis, the department also tracks progress against each year's action plan.

considerations in delivering impact. Table 2.1 presents mission statements by state financial holding companies from around the world that Baiterek could draw lessons from. In Colombia, the focus has been on ensuring distance from political interference and improving corporate governance. In Singapore, the focus has been on professionalizing corporate practices so that Temasek, the state-owned holding company, can serve as an informed and active shareholder catalyzing investment impact on human capital, innovation, and sustainable growth. On the European front, efforts to green the investment agenda and improve the lives of citizens are now driving the strategic plans of the two cited institutions (France's Caisse des Dépôts et Consignations [CDC] and Italy's Cassa Depositi e Prestiti). Rethinking the current mission of Baiterek and grounding it further in quantifiable mandates that include corporate governance and the delivery of ESG impacts could improve the way targets, KPIs, and operations are designed and assessed.

For Baiterek to be more effective as a development tool, the new national and financial sector strategies need to define a clear role for it. The rationale for Baiterek needs to account for market failures, and explain how the state via Baiterek can address these failures and demonstrate additionality. Baiterek should also play a social role via its commercial operations by identifying which segments of the economy and the society need to be prioritized, defining targets and objectives, and setting an impact vision that is quantifiable and can be progressively monitored. Within this context, the Baiterek Board plays a critical role by providing strategic guidance and overseeing the mission implementation by the management. A comprehensive set of objectives and targets needs to be thought through, designed, and revised at intervals as operations grow and reform progresses. Baiterek management then needs to formulate a business plan, design interventions, and establish metrics that make the holding company accountable to the government, Parliament, and the public at large.

TABLE 2.1 Policy objectives of financial holdings: Examples from Colombia, Italy, Singapore, and France

COLOMBIA—GRUPO BICENTENARIO	ITALY—CASSA DEPOSITI E PRESTITI
• Optimize the nation's stock portfolio. • Centralize the property rights of the nation. • Undertake clear and structured corporate governance. • Promote efficiencies in the consolidated management of state entities that provide financial and insurance services.	• Play a decisive role in the growth and sustainable development of Italy. • Make up for the country's delays and achieve a significant economic, social, and environmental impact. • Stay close to and support municipal and rural areas.
SINGAPORE—TEMASEK	FRANCE—CDC
• Serve as an active shareholder and investor. • Serve as a trusted steward. • Invest in human potential. • Catalyze solutions. • Build with courage. • Grow for generations.	• Finance businesses. • Support the housing sector. • Develop regions. • Sustain the environment. • Support the lives of French people.

Sources: Caisse des Dépôts et Consignations, "Our Tasks," https://www.caissedesdepots.fr/en/en/modele-unique/nos-missions; Cassa Depositi e Prestiti, "Governance," https://www.cdp.it/sitointernet/en/governance.page; Temasek, "Our Purpose, Charter, and Values," https://www.temasek.com.sg/en/about-us/our-purpose-charter-values; Grupo Bicentenario, "Mission," https://www.grupobicentenario.gov.co/.
Note: CDC = Caisse des Dépôts et Consignations.

Improving the way in which the state governs its financial assets is instrumental to achieving the objectives of the financial sector strategy. Baiterek remains Kazakhstan's key policy vehicle for financial sector and economic development, but its success may be impeded by the way the state exercises and rolls out its ownership rights. The Corporate Governance Code for Joint Stock Companies has attempted to pave the way to enhancing corporate practices. The code is comprehensive on corporate practices, and Baiterek's compliance scores are quite high. Yet the code fails to provide guidance on the best relation between the state and the holding company. What is of paramount importance for any state property globally, and for Baiterek in particular, is how to minimize political interference in the decision-making process to ensure that the holding company's long-term mandate comes first. As chapter 4 on corporate governance will highlight, strong political representation on the main governing body remains a key concern that will have to be addressed. Of equal concern is the need for greater separation between the oversight and the management functions.

The roles of overseeing and managing state-owned enterprises (SOEs) should be allocated to the most appropriate levels in a command chain extending from the highest levels of government to individual enterprises.[3] This allocation depends first and foremost on clarifying the rationale for state participation in financial services, as well as the related institutional arrangements that support the role of the state (if present) in tackling market failures, closing identified market gaps, and demonstrating additionality, including through crowding in and mobilization of private capital. Clear roles must be assigned in hierarchical order to government (policy formulation), ownership (administration of state interest), boards (oversight and guidance in line with mandate), and management (execution of activities to fulfill the mandate), while preserving operational autonomy of the different entities' functions.

Baiterek has attracted talent from the private sector (for manager positions) and has hired graduates from reputable universities, but staff capacity may still be limited for the task at hand. Professionalizing human resources and providing adequate skill sets for the required tasks is critical for enhancing how Baiterek's government oversight and ownership operate and deliver on their respective mandates. Baiterek employees remain limited by civil service pay scales and recruiting processes, both of which have been identified in interviews as key challenges to upgrading staff skills. Civil servants' pay remains well below that of private sector peers, and this impacts Baiterek's ability to attract and retain qualified employees, especially in key functions such as risk management, internal controls, and internal audit—which appear insufficiently staffed. Understaffing may also be the result of a cumbersome recruitment process. But the staffing issue is not a challenge for Baiterek only. MNE departments dedicated to monitoring Baiterek activities remain understaffed as well. The Concept for the Development of Public Administration until 2030 attempts to deal with both aspects and converges into one simple concept: build a "people first" model for all civil servants, whether they are ministerial or SOE employees.[4] Given the reductions in staff undergone by the State Property Committee, MNE, and other key principles for SOE ownership in the last five years, the Public Administration Reform Strategy 2030 could offer the opportunity to conduct a skill gap analysis that identifies the human resource needs for the renewed Baiterek's mission. In addition, a compensation review based on market benchmarks could further help attract and retain suitable candidates—the pay scale for Baiterek could be aligned with that of NBK and AFR, which tap the same market of financial professionals.

Baiterek has ample margins to develop further as a policy institution. It could achieve this goal via three fundamental steps: redefining the mandate of the institution, streamlining the process that defines its strategy and performance management, and reviewing the efficiency of the monitoring function.

Redefining the mandate of the institution should include a focus on impact, environmental, and additionality considerations. Baiterek's current mandate is broad enough to enable the holding company to spur economic growth via the implementation of the financial policy program priorities. Yet the current role of Baiterek involves a large fiscal agent function for the government, in which it provides interest rate subsidies and buys bonds of local executive bodies. There is a need to graduate Baiterek from this fiscal role and redefine a role grounded in impact and additionality, including environmental considerations and private financial market development.

To successfully establish this new role, Baiterek's strategy must be properly formulated; if a new mandate is to be defined, then the strategy and KPI setting must follow suit. Baiterek's strategy is ultimately the result of a top-down approach, which is not uncommon among SOEs. But the process of bringing together policy priorities is often cumbersome; this process also substantially decreases Baiterek's political independence and interferes with its focus on delivering medium-term impact (as opposed to annual outputs). Streamlining the process for defining KPIs and targets should be done, at a minimum. Even better would be to abolish the annual negotiation of KPIs and targets with ministries (the "owners" of budget funding/financing) and instead provide the KPIs and targets through the Baiterek Board for a four- to five-year period linked to the government's medium-term expenditure framework (MTEF) if Baiterek is channeling fiscal transfers—such as interest rate subsidies. Such KPI and target setting would be aligned with more predictable budgeting and help Baiterek focus on medium-term impacts (outcomes) rather than annual outputs. The MNE ownership department could continue supporting the Baiterek Board in setting the medium-term KPIs and targets.

The final step is to review the performance monitoring of Baiterek and its subsidiaries. Currently, target formulation for performance monitoring is a process that MNE completes in conjunction with the Institute of National Economics. This process could be carried out fully in house if there were sufficient human resources; if not, reallocation of staff should be considered. In addition, individual subsidiary performance has become difficult to unbundle and ascertain. Therefore, the target formulation review should ensure that each subsidiary's contributions to impact can be measured and verified. A key role assigned to MNE is to monitor the performance of SOEs at the level of individual institutions, which is relevant to Baiterek and its separately incorporated subsidiaries.

Table 2.2 shows the suggested actions for enhancing the role of Baiterek as a policy tool.

TABLE 2.2 **Recommendations: Baiterek as a policy tool**

ACTION	RESPONSIBLE ENTITY	EXPECTED RESULT
Update the mandate of Baiterek to include impact on ultimate beneficiaries and markets—including impacts on environmental outcomes—and additionality considerations in impact definition	Cabinet, MNE, Baiterek Board	More accountable impact framework covering climate change agenda
Abolish annual setting and negotiation of KPIs and targets for Baiterek; set the process on a four- to five-year cycle linked to MTEF; align KPIs with augmented/new mandate	Cabinet, MNE	KPIs aligned with augmented mandate and focused on medium-term impact; KPI targets more predictably linked to budget support/financing where needed
Review performance monitoring of Baiterek and its subsidiaries; allow for KPI hierarchy that also enables monitoring of performance at the level of Baiterek subsidiaries	MNE, Baiterek Board, Auditor General Office (and ASPIR)	Robust M&E framework established to assess performance of Baiterek at the subsidiary as well as group level
Review efficiency of the MNE oversight function and assess skill force needs and compensation policy for MNE ownership department	MNE	Enhanced MNE oversight capacity
Review Baiterek's pay scale to enable attraction and retention of talent from among financial sector professionals; consider comparability to NBK and AFR	Cabinet, MNE	Enhanced capacity of human resources to deliver on impact

Source: World Bank.
Note: AFR = Agency for Regulation and Development of the Financial Markets; ASPIR = Agency for Strategic Planning and Reforms; KPI = key performance indicator; M&E = monitoring and evaluation; MNE = Ministry of National Economy; MTEF = medium-term expenditure framework; NBK = National Bank of Kazakhstan.

NOTES

1. During 2017–19, consumer lending grew rapidly at a 15–27 percent rate. In 2021, the consumer and mortgage lending sped up again at 37 percent, becoming the main driver of total credit growth.
2. The seven priorities relate to the development of (i) a strong and successful state; (ii) a sustainable process of democratization and liberalization; (iii) harmony and peace among disparate social, ethnic, and religious groups; (iv) national economy role in international division of labor; (v) strong social policy to ensure social stability and harmony; (vi) being a globally recognized country; and (vii) proactive role in promoting a nuclear nonproliferation regime. See Official Website of the President of Kazakhstan, "Strategies and Programs," https://www.akorda.kz/en/official_documents/strategies_and_programs.
3. This is one of the overarching principles of the World Bank/Organisation for Economic Co-operation and Development (OECD) SOE guidelines (OECD 2015).
4. The strategy builds on past efforts to improve the civil service capability, identifies key current challenges, and recommends solutions. The additional current challenges, not limited to Baiterek, are the lack of proper interaction between citizens and the state, limited effectiveness of strategic planning and reform approaches, functions of the state apparatus that are not focused on the needs of the population and business, the administrative nature of public services, and an ineffective quasi-public sector.

REFERENCE

OECD (Organisation for Economic Co-operation and Development). 2015. *OECD Guidelines on Corporate Governance of State-Owned Enterprises.* 2015 edition. Paris: OECD Publishing. http://dx.doi.org/10.1787/9789264244160-en.

3 Institutional Arrangements and Broader Governance

Ownership reforms of state-owned enterprises (SOEs) seek to clarify the state's role as owner, reduce fragmentation of ownership responsibilities across institutions, and enhance accountability for results. Such reforms should also aim to give boards and management of (financial) SOEs greater autonomy in operational decision-making. A critical goal is to separate the state's ownership functions from its policy-making and regulatory functions, both to sharpen the focus on ownership issues and to minimize the conflicts of interest that may arise when the roles are combined, especially in segments and activities where the private sector is present. Examples of Baiterek subsidiaries that operate in market segments with a private sector presence include the housing finance segment, the agricultural finance segment (Agrarian Credit Corporation), and the fund of funds (Kazyna Capital Management).

The government exercises its ownership rights through different channels that allow for political interference. The term "ownership function" refers to the fundamental rights and normal functions exercised by shareholders; it includes, for instance, the right to nominate (or appoint) members to the board, the right to vote at the general meeting of shareholders, and the right to approve financials. The term "ownership arrangement" refers to the way in which the state organizes itself to exercise its ownership rights over Baiterek. While the sole owner of Baiterek is by law the Ministry of National Economy (MNE), other ministries take part in the active ownership of Baiterek by sitting on the board, by deciding on the holding company's strategic direction, and by overseeing the operations of Baiterek as line ministries. As a result, the Baiterek Board concentrates representation of several ministries and creates a de facto political board that acts as an overseer of the holding company's operations as well as the de facto operational governing body. In addition, the government has assigned the State Property Committee the role of managing the sale of state assets.

The rationale behind the establishment of state-owned holding companies is to separate the state ownership function from the politically independent management. This arrangement of state ownership should in turn permit depoliticization and greater operational independence for the SOEs/development finance institutions (DFIs) under the holding company umbrella. The ministerial presence on the board of the holding company is not unusual; for example, the ownership entity in Peru includes five ministers on the five-member board. However, in several countries, such boards are expected to have a technical skill set and to be independent. The board of Samruk Kazyna, the national holding company for state-owned nonfinancial enterprises, was designed with these expectations in mind, and Baiterek could consider following a similar model. The recently constituted Grupo Bicentenario, the holding company for state financial services in Colombia, reflects a long political process and represents a new way to interpret and manage state assets: to reach consensus, parties adopt best corporate governance practices, and the operations of the state-owned financial institutions (SOFIs) are insulated from political influence (see box 3.1).

If the government were to consider a revision of Baiterek's board composition and overall organizational structure, it could draw on relevant good practices. While compliance with the Code for Corporate Governance seems to have improved at both the holding company and subsidiary levels, the code provides less guidance on groupwide practices. These relate to the development of uniform group policies and realistic expectations for the subsidiary boards. Groupwide governance policies are also more effective when supported by embedded procedures that keep practices consistent throughout the group, and for this reason governance units are often formed. Baiterek could consider the development of a dedicated unit that monitors transition progress.

It is also important to note that boards of *closely held* subsidiaries often have different governance needs than subsidiaries that have mixed ownership or parents, or that are stand-alone banks. For closely held subsidiary boards, formal independence remains relevant; such boards must also have sufficient knowledge and experience to perform their oversight role, sufficient diversity of views, and the ability to effectively challenge subsidiary management. Best practice suggests that parent boards be capable of accurately tracking subsidiary governance.

Board committees can also contribute to improving the effectiveness of the accountability framework. About a decade ago, the Italian capital market regulator introduced the requirement that audit committees issue an opinion on suitability (terms and strategic alignment) of large transactions. This requirement has enhanced the quality of decision-making and shielded members of committees from potential fiduciary duty liabilities. Baiterek committees (on impact, risk, audit, and human resources; see a detailed discussion in chapter 4)

The Colombian case: Grupo Bicentenario

The recently created Grupo Bicentenario (GB), a financial holding company for state-owned financial institutions (SOFIs) reporting to the Ministry of Finance (Ministerio de Hacienda y Crédito Público [MHCP]), is the third largest financial group in Colombia. The MHCP should appoint permanent boards and managers to the GB with strong financial expertise, and it should ramp up operations (especially around board appointments to the SOFIs). The creation of GB provides an opportunity to conduct an ambitious review of the SOFIs' rationale and operations and to prepare a strategy that restructures the group to increase efficiency, avoid duplication, and ensure alignment with policy objectives. Having reincorporated SOFIs into joint stock companies, the MHCP is working on developing a transparent dividend policy process, a monitoring and performance evaluation framework, and a corporate governance policy.

Sources: Bernal Devia 2019; Grupo Bicentenario establishing documents and website, https://www.grupobicentenario.gov.co/.

should be composed solely of independent members, and they should issue opinions on the proposed actions/transactions in their purview to safeguard their independence and integrity and increase the political board's accountability. Documentation of these actions should be available to the Auditor General Office (AGO) and responsible parliamentary committees as the primary enforcers of Baiterek's accountability.

Defining an optimal economic relation with stakeholders and shareholders has also proved to be an effective accountability solution. An effective trend that has emerged especially for development banks of a recent constitution is the strengthening of their relations with key shareholders and stakeholders. This strengthening is especially relevant now that Baiterek is reaching more customers and has increased its debt volumes, and the debt holders with significant debt positions need to play their role within the accountability mechanisms. Yet stewardship by institutional investors of international credibility has born little fruit, given the passive role that those institutional investors play through a debt investment position. The entry of a passive equity investor such as a typical international financial institution would be the next step in accountability additionality; it could exert discipline in impact and performance monitoring, with divestment and exit as the ultimate enforcement tools (since they can act as a credible threat and may truly affect the stewardship of the DFI). Stewardship benefits most when an institutional (impact) investor becomes an active shareholder by entering the capital structure as a strategic investor. There are immediate accountability additionalities that the presence of active equity holders other than the state can bring to the table. For this reason, many newly established DFIs have been constituted with minority institutional investor capital since inception (for example, the Nigerian Development Bank or the Colombian Infrastructure Bank). Practices at the board level, the general assembly level, and the reporting level need to align to be more representative of the new capital structure, and this alignment in turn pushes the institution to adopt better governance practices.

The ownership structure of Baiterek appears centralized and decentralized at the same time. While the only legal owner of Baiterek is the MNE, the process of formulating key performance indicators (KPIs) and targets reveals a concerted ministerial effort that defines expectations of Baiterek's operations. The influence of the line ministries goes beyond sectoral policies. They play an active role in defining Baiterek's strategy and KPIs. But the strategy and KPI targets should ultimately be the task of the legal owner (MNE), in conjunction with a supporting board of directors composed of professional and independent actors. While this top-down approach trickles down national priorities and sectoral needs into Baiterek's operations, it fragments ownership and reduces the arm's length relationship of the state with the holding company.

International practices have focused over the years on developing clarifying documents that elaborate the relationship between the owner and its companies. Kazakhstan has worked effectively in clearly splitting the SOE portfolio into the real economy and financial services. However, at this juncture it would be useful to formally clarify what role the line ministries should play to create a balance that enhances the centralization of ownership in favor of the MNE.

It is therefore recommended that the relationship between Baiterek and the government of Kazakhstan be clarified via an ownership policy. The ownership policy should clarify both the government's justification for being in certain segments of the economy (rationale of state ownership) and the dividend opportunities. The 2015 dividend decree imposed on Baiterek requires it to transfer 70 percent of the revenues to the state, which is quite high compared to international practice. This policy has an impact on operations, strategic guidance, and reinvestment opportunities. In fact, the revision of the dividend policy could be another source of greater independence for Baiterek from sideways influence by ministries. For example, if Baiterek is expected to grow and scale up some areas of its support—such as market-friendly credit guarantees—over the next four to five years, the dividend payout policy could be adjusted such that recapitalized profits enable this growth, and the budget fund transferred in the medium-term expenditure framework is lowered together with the stake of line ministries in direct negotiation of Baiterek KPIs and targets. The board composition requires more realistic expectations in line with Organisation for Economic Co-operation and Development (OECD) SOE guidelines, which suggest that the state should act as an informed and active owner that grants operational autonomy to Baiterek to achieve defined objectives and refrains from intervening in its management (OECD 2015).[1]

A well-designed performance contract is an effective tool that can enhance the relationship between the holding company's management and the government by clarifying the focus on impacts. Greater emphasis on performance contracts for top executives could be considered. Performance contracts are meant to hold management accountable to targets and key performance indicators, and their design continues to evolve (Thorne and Du Toit 2009). Baiterek has begun to draft and sign performance contracts with key executives. The MNE monitors activities annually and is required to assess Baiterek operations every three years.[2] Performance contracts have had mixed results in the past due to several factors, including targets that are hard for outsiders to evaluate or easy for the firm to achieve, high number of and frequent changes to targets, and lack of accountability mechanisms to enforce contracts (Simpson 2013; Simpson and Buabeng 2013). Three aspects of international good practice should be considered by Baiterek in improving performance contracts. First, performance contracts should include fewer KPIs (five to eight KPIs at most) with targets along financial, customer, operational, and organizational dimensions. Second, targets of each KPI should be benchmarked against comparable international peers, and management should be responsible for proper implementation of KPIs and for reporting them to the market. Third, business performance reviews should be conducted regularly to identify any major shortcomings and to draft action plans to further improve performance (World Bank 2014).

Quantifying policy obligations and defining better performance indicators can provide more focus and clarity in the way Baiterek operations are rolled out and performance contracts are designed. The current challenges in performance monitoring relate to the quantification of policy obligations, which tend to blur into commercial budget considerations; this ambiguity undermines efforts to balance commercial and socioeconomic (including environmental) objectives. In the same vein, the current performance contracting could better capture through the indicators employed the developmental role that Baiterek should play. The Korea Development Bank performance agreement can shed light on both quantification and indicator design (box 3.2).

Korea Development Bank

In the Republic of Korea, performance agreements for the head of state-owned enterprises were introduced in 2014. Annual performance evaluations are conducted by the Finanial Service Commission. Evaluation indicators are both quantitative and qualitative and relate to general management functions as well as key projects. Management indicators relate to strategy implementation, financial performance, human resource management, and customer satisfaction. Project indicators include attainment of funding level goals, project financial performance, loan delinquency levels, support for corporate restructuring, and small and medium enterprise growth. The performance evaluation report is used to determine bonuses for management and employees and to make decisions regarding chief executive officer continuity.[a] For example, the strategy goals of the latest strategy (2019–23) are grounded in strategic tasks against which management performance is assessed (table B3.2.1).

TABLE B3.2.1 **Strategic goals and tasks of Korea Development Bank**

STRATEGIC GOALS	STRATEGIC TASKS
Lead innovation and growth	• Foster new industries and technologies
	• Become a leading venture capital platform
	• Strengthen the role as a venture capital supplier
Support the reshaping of the industrial ecosystem	• Help the mainstay industries enhance their competitiveness
	• Facilitate the generational transition in corporate leadership
Enhance the competitiveness of global and investment banking business	• Expand the operational base for global operations
	• Increase profitability of global operations
	• Globalize investment bank operations and provide more support through policy financing
Pioneer new areas of policy finance	• Actively seek out new demands for policy finance
	• Prepare for a new economic era for the Korean peninsula
Build stable and sustainable operational foundation	• Pursue bank-wide digital transformation
	• Build on the capacity for stable revenue generation
	• Introduce innovation to the organization and internal process

Source: KDB 2021.
a. Korea Development Bank website, https://www.kdb.co.kr/index.jsp.

The project development index currently being tested by the Development Bank of Kazakhstan is a step in the right direction. This new tool being used in the holding company and in the region is not supposed to be a key criterion, but it is being designed to have weight in the decision-making process and could be leveraged in performance contracts. The project development index is similar to an economic development index, but its exact methodology has not yet been disclosed.

There are two financial companies owned by the state that Baiterek could consider including in its portfolio. The investment companies are Samruk-Kazyna Invest and Kazakh Invest. Both companies have representatives in each region and aim to finance regional investment projects, but the companies do not have financial instruments to attract foreign investments. They have regional offices and can incorporate investment functions into their regional offices. In principle, Baiterek Holding should integrate all (at least domestic/non–Astana International Financial Centre [AIFC]) DFIs within its structure to foster best-practice governance for such state institutions and companies and promote accountability for impact.[3] This would also potentially include the noncommercial state-owned joint stock company for life insurance, annuity insurance, and accident insurance.[4] Together with export and import insurance and agricultural insurance, integrating this company into Baiterek could help develop an insurance-focused SOFI that could usefully complement market development operations and penetration of catastrophic insurance—which is a big development challenge for Kazakhstan (World Bank 2020).

Several government entities as well as the private financial audit profession play a role in overseeing Baiterek and enforcing accountability in its operations. After taking the leading role in policy formulation by coordinating Baiterek's KPI formulation, KPI targets, and timelines of action, the MNE also performs an oversight function for Baiterek from its position as sole legal owner. Interviews reveal that staffing gaps and salary structures need to be addressed to attract and retain professional staff. In addition to MNE, the AGO also performs a complementary oversight function and enforces accountability in Baiterek's operations. The AGO has undergone downsizing and is currently making efforts to close the auditing cycle and overcome delays related to the schedule of analysis—for example, by August 2022, Baiterek's 2021 annual report had not yet been published. The delays and capacity gaps in the work of the AGO have an impact on the role of the Parliamentary Committee on Finance and Economics, which is the ultimate public enforcement arm if financial reporting inconsistencies are detected and the measured impacts are doubtful. The weakness of the financial reporting analysis also has an impact on the working of the Public Debt Management Office, the MNE Budget Committee, and the State Property Committee—the last of which has a key role to play in the sale of state assets. Furthermore, all Baiterek entities are subject to external financial audit, as is the holding company itself. Beyond reliably auditing the financial statement, auditing professionals should include statements on Baiterek's reported impact against its published KPIs and targets.

Suggested actions for improving governance, along with responsible entities and the expected results, are shown in table 3.1.

TABLE 3.1 Recommendations: Institutional arrangements and broader governance

ACTION	RESPONSIBLE ENTITY	EXPECTED RESULT
Develop a policy to define ownership rationale for state-owned holding company and relation between state and Baiterek	Cabinet and MNE	Enacted ownership policy in line with best international practices
Revise performance contracts	MNE (and Baiterek Board for managers)	Improved performance and accountability of independent board members and professional managers

Source: World Bank.
Note: MNE = Ministry of National Economy.

NOTES

1. The scope of the ownership policy in several jurisdictions has gone beyond one single sector where the state is present, and has cross-cut the SOE portfolio to focus on state commercial operations, irrespective of their real or financial sectoral focus. It is suggested that one policy should cover all the commercial activities of the state, including Baiterek.
2. A useful element of performance monitoring is benchmarking against industry standards and comparators. This element helps identify gaps and areas for improvement. It is still underdeveloped in many emerging market countries, but ownership entities are beginning to strive to benchmark performance against appropriate peers, whether domestic or foreign.
3. AIFC is a regional financial hub in Astana, Kazakhstan, that officially launched on July 5, 2018. The constitutional statute "On the Astana International Financial Centre," approved on December 7, 2015, provides a legal framework for the functioning of the AIFC as well as a favorable environment for its participants.
4. See the company website at https://www.gak.kz/about.

REFERENCES

Bernal Devia, S. L. 2019. "Análisis del nuevo holding estatal de servicios financieros en Colombia" [Analysis of the new state financial services holding in Colombia]. Working paper, New Granada Military University, Bogotá. https://repository.unimilitar.edu.co /handle/10654/36181.

KDB (Korea Development Bank). 2021. "2021 Annual Report." https://vpr.hkma.gov.hk/statics /assets/doc/200110/ar_21/ar_21_eng.pdf.

OECD (Organisation for Economic Co-operation and Development). 2015. *OECD Guidelines on Corporate Governance of State-Owned Enterprises*. 2015 edition. Paris: OECD Publishing. http://dx.doi.org/10.1787/9789264244160-en.

Simpson, S. N. Y. 2013. "Performance Contract and Performance Evaluation of State-Owned Enterprises: Insights from the Goal Setting Theory." *Journal of Public Administration and Governance* 3 (2): 22–39.

Simpson, S. N. Y., and T. Buabeng. 2013. "Performance Contract and Performance of Public Enterprises: A Study of the Implementation Processes." *Journal of Public Administration and Governance* 3 (2): 10–21.

Thorne, J., and C. Du Toit. 2009. "A Macro-Framework for Successful Development Banks." *Development Southern Africa* 26 (5): 677–94.

World Bank. 2014. *Corporate Governance of State-Owned Enterprises: A Toolkit*. Washington, DC: World Bank.

World Bank. 2020. "Kazakhstan: Southeast Europe and Central Asia Catastrophe Risk Insurance Facility." Implementation Completion and Results Report ICR5056, World Bank, Washington, DC. https://documents1.worldbank.org/curated/en/418831594399210904 /pdf/Kazakhstan-Southeast-Europe-and-Central-Asia-Catastrophe-Risk-Insurance -Facility-Project.pdf.

4 Governance of Baiterek Holding JSC

This chapter is structured in three sections. The first section reviews key governance principles under the Organisation for Economic Development and Co-operation (OECD) guidelines on corporate governance of state-owned enterprises (SOEs) as they apply to Baiterek Holding Joint Stock Company (JSC). The second section provides a benchmarking of the governance structure of state-owned financial holding companies in selected advanced and emerging markets. Based on this analysis, the third section provides detailed recommendations for the reform of the governance structure of Baiterek Holding JSC.

OECD GUIDELINES ON CORPORATE GOVERNANCE OF STATE-OWNED ENTERPRISES

The OECD guidelines on corporate governance of SOEs rest on the fundamental principle that the state should act as an informed and active owner (OECD 2015). That is, the state should ensure that the governance of SOEs is carried out in a transparent and accountable manner, with a high degree of professionalism and effectiveness. Based on this principle, the guidelines stipulate that the exercise of ownership rights should be clearly identified within the state administration. The exercise of ownership rights should be centralized in a single ownership entity or, if this is not possible, carried out by a coordinating body. This ownership entity should have the capacity and competencies to effectively carry out its duties (see chapter 3).

The guidelines stipulate that the government should allow SOEs full operational autonomy to achieve their defined objectives and refrain from intervening in SOE management. In particular, the government as a shareholder should avoid redefining SOE objectives in a nontransparent manner. The guidelines further stipulate that the state should let SOE boards exercise their responsibilities and should respect their independence. These guidelines fully apply to Baiterek Holding JSC and its subsidiaries as SOEs.

BENCHMARKING WITH STATE-OWNED FINANCIAL HOLDING COMPANIES IN SELECTED COUNTRIES

This section examines the governance structure of state-owned financial holding companies in selected advanced and emerging markets as benchmarks for Baiterek. The benchmarking analysis covers Temasek Holding in Singapore; Khazanah National in Malaysia; Caisse des Dépôts et Consignations (CDC) in France; Cassa Depositi e Prestiti (CDP) in Italy; Banco Nacional de Desenvolvimento (BNDES) in Brazil; and Development Bank of South Africa (DBSA).

Temasek Holding (Singapore)

Temasek Holding was incorporated under the Singapore Companies Act in 1974 with the responsibility to own and commercially manage investments and assets previously owned by the government of Singapore. Temasek is 100 percent owned by the Ministry of Finance and is accountable to the ministry. Temasek's sole shareholder is the Minister of Finance Inc., a corporate body established under the Singapore Minister of Finance Incorporation Act. However, under Singapore's Constitution and laws, neither the president nor the minister of finance is involved in investment, exit, or other business decisions, except in the protection of Temasek's own past reserves. All investment and operational decisions are made by Temasek's Board and management. The only exception is that Temasek's Board is required by the Singapore Constitution to seek the president's approval before a draw occurs on Temasek's past reserves. Companies in Temasek's portfolio are guided and managed by their respective boards and management, and Temasek Holding does not direct their business decisions or operations.

The Temasek Board and management team are composed of independent professionals with extensive experience across various industries in both the private and the public sectors in Singapore and abroad. The minister of finance is responsible for the appointment, renewal, or removal of board members, with the concurrence of the president. The board currently consists of 14 members. The board appoints the CEO of the holding company and the CEOs of the SOEs owned by the holding company, also with the concurrence of the president.

Khazanah National (Malaysia)

Khazanah National was incorporated as a limited liability company under the Companies Act in 1993 to be an investment-holding arm of the government of Malaysia and to effect the separation of the ownership functions and the supervision functions for SOEs. The original mission of Khazanah was to promote economic growth and make strategic investments on behalf of the government. Its mandate was updated in 2004 to include a more proactive investment approach, one that enhances the performance of existing holdings while seeking opportunities in new economic sectors and geographies.

Except for one share owned by the federal land commissioner, all other shares are owned by the Minister of Finance Inc.—a corporate body established by the Minister of Finance Incorporation Act of 1957. The Incorporation Act assigns the minister of finance the responsibility for finance as the body corporate under the name "Minister of Finance." Khazanah owns shares in more than

50 government-linked corporations in which the government has a direct controlling stake; these are in a variety of sectors.

Khazanah is managed by a nine-member board of directors, consisting of experts from both the public and the private sectors. The board is chaired by the prime minister and minister of finance and assisted by Executive and Audit Committees. The minister of finance therefore acts both as the sole owner of Khazanah as the body corporate of Minister of Finance Inc. and as cochair of the board of Khazanah. The senior management team is responsible for implementing and delivering on strategic and corporate objectives and is made up of 19 professionals with financial sector experience.

Caisse des Dépôts et Consignations (France)

The Caisse des Dépôts et Consignations was established by the French Parliament as a state-owned financial institution in 1816. The CDC has four core activities: The first, the Banque des Territoires, was launched in 2018 and offers consulting and financial solutions in the form of loans and investments to meet the needs of local authorities, social housing organizations, local public companies, and the legal profession. The second, the Directorate for Pensions and Solidarity, manages 65 pension and solidarity funds and plans. The third, the Asset Management Department, manages financial investments in bonds, shares, unlisted companies, property, and forests. The fourth, the Strategic Investments Department, is in charge of acquisition, creation, and divestiture operations in around 20 companies in which the CDC is the reference shareholder. In addition, the CDC has two specialized subsidiaries: BPI France, which offers financing through loans, guarantees, equity investments, and consulting to companies at all stages of their development (and which has supported more than 300,000 companies since its creation); and La Poste Group, which offers banking services to the French population as a local player rooted in regions.

The governance of the CDC is based on two key principles: independence of the Supervisory Board and autonomy of the chief executive officer. The Supervisory Board is responsible for overseeing the management of the group and the CEO's decisions. It is composed of 16 members: five members of Parliament (three deputies and two senators); five members appointed by Parliament; two representatives from the CDC's staff; the director general of the Treasury; and three members appointed by the state. The rule of gender parity must be respected. The Supervisory Board is supported by the General Secretariat. It has five specialized committees: the Audit and Risk Committee, the Savings Committee, the Investments Committee, the Appointments and Compensation Committee, and the Strategy Committee. The chairperson of the board is a member of Parliament.

The CEO presides over the Executive Committee, which is the CDC's main governance body. The CEO is appointed by the president for a period of five years following parliamentary approval. The CEO decides on the strategy of the CDC, monitors its operational performance, and ensures that the services offered meet client, partner, and user needs.

Cassa Depositi e Prestiti (Italy)

The Cassa Depositi e Prestiti was established by the Parliament of the Kingdom of Sardinia in 1850, initially to mobilize capital received by the state through private savings channels for public utility works. Following the unification of Italy in 1863, the CDP gradually expanded its role as a financial holding company under the authority of the Ministry of the Treasury. It was transformed into a state-owned joint stock company in 2003. The Cassa Group encompasses seven companies: (i) CDP Equity, responsible for making equity investments in Italian companies with the objective of achieving growth, competitiveness, and internationalization; (ii) CDP Reti, responsible for managing equity investments in strategic infrastructures in the gas and electricity sectors; (iii) CDP Industria, responsible for managing investments in major Italian industrial corporates; (iv) Fintecna, responsible for managing equity investments and for specialized management of liquidation processes; (v) Simest, responsible for supporting the growth of Italian companies through the internationalization of their business; (vi) CDP Immobiliare, responsible for investing in property development, and (vii) CDP Immobiliare SGR, responsible for supporting housing policies, enhancement of public assets, and growth in the tourism sector.

The Board of Directors of the CDP guides and directs the group's activities, with the support of internal committees and the supervision of control bodies. The board consists of nine members, including the director general of the Treasury, the accountant general of the state, and representatives of the regions, provinces, and municipalities. A magistrate of the Court of Auditors attends the meetings of the board. The board is supported in its decisions by five internal committees with consulting and advisory functions, including (i) the Risk and Sustainability Committee; (ii) the Appointments Committee; (iii) the Compensation Committee; (iv) the Related Parties Committee; and (v) the Support Noncontrolling Shareholders Committee. In particular, the Risk and Sustainability Committee performs functions of control and provides guidance on risk management and sustainability.

The control bodies include the Board of Auditors Supervisory Board and the Parliamentary Supervisory Committee. The Board of Auditors Supervisory Board is composed of five standing auditors and two alternates. The Parliamentary Supervisory Committee is composed of parliamentary members (representatives of the Chamber of Deputies and the Senate) and nonparliamentary members (representatives of the Council of the State and State Audit Court).

Banco Nacional de Desenvolvimento (Brazil)

The Banco Nacional de Desenvolvimento is the main financing agent for development in Brazil. Since its foundation in 1952, BNDES has played a fundamental role in stimulating the expansion of industry and infrastructure in the country. In the course of its development, its operations have evolved to include support to exports, technological innovation, sustainable socioeconomic development, and the modernization of public administration.

BNDES has two integral subsidiaries: FINAME and BNDESPAR. FINAME resources are earmarked for the financing, purchase, sale, and export of Brazilian machinery and equipment, as well as import of goods of the same nature produced overseas. BNDESPAR is a business corporation responsible for capitalization operations of undertakings controlled by private groups while abiding by BNDES plans and policies. In addition, BNDESPAR is responsible for helping to strengthen Brazil's capital market by expanding the offer of securities and democratizing the ownership of company capital.

BNDES has a corporate board of directors that is controlled by the Fiscal Council, composed of representatives of external agencies. It is also subject to the Advisory Council, composed of representatives of the government and civil society. As a financial institution, BNDES is subject to inspection by Brazil's central bank and the norms and resolutions of the National Monetary Council. In addition, its accounts are inspected by the Federal Court of Accounts, an auxiliary entity to the National Congress, while its processes are audited by the Office of the Comptroller General.

The members of the board of directors are elected by the General Assembly of BNDES. There are no requirements concerning the independence of board members. The board has broad responsibilities for overall corporate strategy and oversight of operations, the establishment and oversight of subsidiaries, and appointment of members of the Audit Committee, Compensation Committee, and Eligibility Committee. The Fiscal Council is responsible for overseeing the actions of the board, including approval of the annual work plan, review of financial statements, review of internal control reports, and review of the annual report. The Audit Committee expresses an opinion on the hiring and dismissal of independent auditors of BNDES and its subsidiaries, assesses the effectiveness of internal and independent audits, and produces the Annual Audit Committee Report.

Development Bank of South Africa

The Development Bank of South Africa is a government-owned development finance institution established under the Development Bank of Southern Africa Act of 1997. Its mandate is to promote economic development and growth, human resource development, and institutional capacity building by mobilizing financial and other resources from the national and international private and public sectors for sustainable development projects and programs in South Africa and the wider African continent. DBSA has no subsidiaries.

The Ministry of Finance acts as the sole shareholder of DBSA. The constitution and conduct of the DBSA Board of Directors is governed by the DBSA Act and further regulated by the Public Finance Management Act and the principles of the King IV Report. The members of the board of directors are appointed by the minister of finance from the private and public sectors based on their academic background and professional experience. As of 2023, the board consists of two executive directors and eight independent non-executive directors, one of whom is the board chair. The two executive directors are the chief executive officer and the chief financial officer of DBSA, and are also members of the management board. There is no requirement for the executive directors to be politically independent.

The board has broad responsibilities for overseeing the management of DBSA. It comprises six committees, specifically on audit and risk, credit and investment, human resources and remuneration, infrastructure delivery and knowledge, social and ethics, and nomination.

Evaluation of selected holding companies' adherence to the OECD guidelines

Among the state-owned financial holdings under review, Temasek adheres most closely to the OECD guidelines. Its board and management team are composed entirely of professionals from the private and the public sectors and do not include political appointees, thus ensuring the independence of the holding company and insulating it from political influence. The Minister of Finance Inc. is responsible for nominating and removing board members subject to approval by the president. Under the Constitution, the minister of finance and the president are not involved in Temasek's investment, exit, and business decisions.

Khazanah National adheres less closely to the guidelines. As in the case of Temasek, the board and the management team are composed of professionals from the private and the public sectors. However, the board is chaired by the prime minister and the minister of finance; thus the holding company is less insulated from political influence than Temasek.

The Caisse des Dépôts et Consignations adheres less closely to the guidelines than either Temasek or Khazanah National. Of its 16 board members, five are representatives from Parliament, which reduces the holding company's political independence.

The Cassa Depositi e Prestiti also adheres less closely to the guidelines than Temasek or Khazanah National. Three of its nine board members are representatives of the regions, provinces, and municipalities, which likewise reduces the holding company's political independence.

The Banco Nacional de Desenvolvimento and the Development Bank of South Africa also adhere less closely to the OECD guidelines than either Temasek or Khazanah National. BNDES does not specify any requirement that board members be politically independent, and while the majority of DBSA board members are independent non-executive directors, there is no requirement for political independence of the executive directors on the board.

RECOMMENDATIONS FOR REFORMING THE GOVERNANCE STRUCTURE OF BAITEREK HOLDING

The current governance structure of Baiterek Holding does not adhere to the OECD guidelines for the governance of SOEs and falls short of international best practice. Baiterek's Board is currently political, chaired by the prime minister, and only three of its 10 members are required to be politically independent. The legislation governing the management of quasi-fiscal institutions will need to be fundamentally revised with the objective of ensuring sufficient independence of SOE management and insulating it from political interference.

There are essentially three main options going forward to improve Baiterek's governance. In the current institutional country context, options 1 and 2 could work better. Option 3 is considered second-best.

- *The first option makes Baiterek's Board of Directors fully politically independent while raising the ownership unit status (currently at the Ministry of National Economy [MNE]) to the level of the prime minister.* Under this option, the prime minster (in coordination with all relevant ministries) provides guidance to Baiterek's boards on vision, key objectives, and results, as they stem from the national development strategy. The main accountability mechanism through the Parliamentary Committee on Finance and Economics and the Auditor General Office (AGO) stays, but it is strengthened by periodic independent evaluations of development impact conducted or commissioned by the AGO or the Agency for Strategic Planning and Reforms (ASPIR) in line with its mandate. This includes Baiterek's greater data production and disclosure and evaluations by nongovernmental organizations (NGOs), markets, and the global community (see chapter 8).

- *The second option, perhaps more politically feasible, changes the composition of the board of directors so that independent directors represent the majority.* This option is elaborated at length in the following paragraph. Under this option, the state's ownership policy, including the guidance based on the national development strategy, is directly exercised by the board, while the boards of Baiterek subsidiaries are isolated from political influence by having only independent board members. No operational approvals are raised to the level of Baiterek's Board, including approvals of large investments, financial decisions, or firing and hiring of staff, among others. The board would play a more passive role than currently, and the MNE staff from the Baiterek ownership unit could be moved to the Board Secretariat. The main accountability mechanism through the Parliamentary Committee on Finance and Economics and the AGO is strengthened and coupled with periodic independent evaluations of development impact conducted or commissioned by AGO or ASPIR in line with its mandate, including greater data production and disclosure and evaluations by NGOs, markets, and the global community (see chapter 8).
- *The third option changes the composition of the board to include properly protected civil servants, who represent the state on the Baiterek Board as politically independent representatives of the public, alongside international independent directors or other non–civil service independent directors.* This option requires a strong civil service code and protections for senior public servants, which currently do not exist in Kazakhstan and may not be established in the short to medium term.

Under the second option, the Baiterek Board could be composed of nine directors, the majority of them independent. The nine directors would include the prime minister (board chair), the minister of national economy, the minister of finance, the representative of the presidential office, and five independent directors. The independent directors would be recruited from the private and nongovernmental sectors—both domestic and international cadres—through an open international competition. The competitive selection process would be managed by a reputable international private recruitment company. The "fit, proper, and independence" tests of the selected candidates would be carried out by a reputable international private integrity due diligence (IDD) company. This testing is critical to increasing the integrity and strengthening the political independence of the board and should be considered as a regular budget expense for Baiterek conducted by the ownership function. Independent board members would be recruited for a five-year nonrenewable term.

Board members should be selected based on transparent criteria related to academic background and professional experience in a mix that reflects the breadth of all Baiterek business lines: candidates should have experience in commercial finance, development (double bottom line) finance, and provision of financial service subsidies, along with complementary sectoral experience corresponding to main sectoral business lines of Baiterek. Candidates should hold a master's degree or equivalent in economics, finance, and/or corporate law and should have at least 15 years of experience in at least one of the following fields: (i) management of a state financial sector holding company; (ii) management of privatization of state-owned financial institutions; (iii) economic analysis for investment projects, including estimation of project economic rate of return and project impact based on international best practice; and (iv) design, targeting, and management of subsidies for financial institutions and services while minimizing market distortions.

The responsibilities of the board of directors could be as follows:

- Discuss and approve the holding company's consolidated strategy and business plan.
- Approve the development and business plans of subsidiaries.
- Approve the semiannual activity reports of subsidiaries.
- Design and approve the consolidated risk, compliance, and internal audit framework.
- Approve group-level policies, such as sustainability/ESG (environmental, social, and governance) and set consolidated targets.
- Monitor the performance of the group against the established criteria and strategies.
- Approve the financial and nonfinancial information to be disclosed at the consolidated level.
- Approve the holding company's annual report.
- Appoint and remove the key executives at the Baiterek Holding level.
- Determine the remuneration policies for Baiterek and the principles applicable for groupwide remuneration policies.

The board of directors would establish specialized board committees composed solely of independent directors (consistent with OECD SOE governance principles [OECD 2015]). Committees would have the following responsibilities:

- The *Impact Committee* would be responsible for advising the board on the approval of Baiterek's impact measurement framework, covering both beneficiaries and market creation, and for performance reviews of the delivered impact.
- The *Risk, Compliance, and Safeguards Committee* would be responsible for advising the board on aspects related to Baiterek's integrated risk management across all types of risk (financial, enterprise, impact-related) and the management of conflicts of interest; on anti-corruption and anti–money laundering and combating the financing of terrorism (AML/CFT) policies and measures; and on any supervisory requirements that Baiterek or its subsidiaries might face on a consolidated or individual level. The committee would also be responsible for recommending to the board the approval of Baiterek's Environmental and Social Management System and would receive reports on the implementation of the framework on a groupwide basis.
- The *Audit Committee* would be responsible for overseeing the internal audit function of the holding company, including proposing the chief internal audit officer to the board, approving the audit plan, receiving the internal audit reports directly from the internal auditor, and organizing the annual external audit.
- The *Remuneration and Compensation Committee* would be responsible for advising the board on the remuneration and appointment policies, proposing the annual remuneration system to the board, and advising the board on Baiterek's procedures and its appointment of any key function holders.

Baiterek's management board would be composed solely of professional senior managers from the private and nongovernment sectors. Members of the management board would be recruited through an open international competition managed by a reputable international recruitment company. Selected candidates would be subject to a fit, proper, and political independence test administered by a reputable international IDD company. This testing is critical to ensure the integrity and political independence of the management board and should be considered as a regular budget expense for the holding company. Note that the role of an IDD company is investigative and is different from that of a headhunting company, which seeks to identify potential candidates suitable for a given position. The investigative role of the IDD company extends to individuals and entities with close connections to the candidate under consideration. Management board members would be recruited for a term of four to five years, renewable by the board. To properly separate the oversight and management functions of Baiterek Holding, the CEO (or other management board members) would no longer sit on the board of directors. The same change should be applied to boards of directors and management of subsidiaries. These reforms could be phased in gradually or implemented on a pilot basis selectively across the holding company and subsidiaries.

The responsibilities of the management board would be as follows:

- Review development and business plans prepared by subsidiaries and submit them to the board of directors for approval.
- Review the semiannual activity reports prepared by subsidiaries and submit them to the board of directors for approval.
- Process the capital contributions from the holding company to the subsidiaries; process the payments for dividends, privatization, and exit proceeds from the subsidiaries to the holding company; and make decisions about large intragroup lending and submit them to the Risk Committee for approval.
- Comply with all the supervisory requirements of the Agency for Regulation and Development of the Financial Markets under the oversight of the Risk, Compliance, and Safeguards Committee.
- Execute all measures related to conflict of interest, anti-corruption, and AML/CFT as directed by the Risk, Compliance, and Safeguards Committee.
- Prepare Baiterek's Environmental and Social Management System and submit it to the Risk, Compliance, and Safeguards Committee for approval.
- Prepare Baiterek's impact strategy (including contribution, attribution, measurement, and verification approaches) and its assessment covering both beneficiaries and market creation and submit it to the Impact Committee for approval.
- Prepare Baiterek's annual report and submit it to the board of directors for approval.

The appointment of subsidiaries' boards of directors and management needs to respect the same logic of separating the oversight from management functions. Namely, the supervisory boards of subsidiaries need to comprise only independent members from the nongovernmental or private sector, appointed by Baiterek Holding's Board of Directors. These candidates need to be vetted by an IDD company and match the expertise required by the subsidiary's business model (commercial, impact, agent); see more details in chapter 6.

Baiterek will be expected to strengthen its internal control functions. The current risk management function may need to be reinforced to ensure that it can properly oversee groupwide risks, particularly those assumed by the subsidiaries. The current model (based on formulating Baiterek's risk appetite framework) of setting groupwide policies while managing a limited number of risks (such as counterparty credit lines, foreign exchange exposures, or intragroup funding) should be expanded to ensure that sufficient resources are allocated to

TABLE 4.1 Recommendations: Governance of Baiterek Holding JSC

ACTION	RESPONSIBLE ENTITY	EXPECTED RESULT
Reform board of holding company		
Option 1: Make the board of directors completely politically independent while raising the ownership unit to the level of the prime minister	PM and MNE	Adherence to OECD SOE corporate governance principles
		Full independence of holding company management and its insulation from political interference
Option 2: Change the composition of the board of directors so that independent directors become the majority	PM and MNE	Partial adherence to OECD SOE corporate governance principles
		Reduced political interference in holding company management while ownership and oversight functions are kept closer to Baiterek and subsidiaries
Include only independent directors in the specialized committees of the holding company's board	PM and MNE	Reduced political interference in Baiterek management
Conduct "fit, proper, and independence" tests of independent directors through a private international IDD company; cost of external IDD company should be considered as a regular budget expense of Baiterek	PM and MNE	Integrity of independent directors

Source: World Bank.
Note: IDD = integrity due diligence; MNE = Ministry of National Economy; OECD = Organisation for Economic Co-operation and Development; PM = prime minister; SOE = state-owned enterprise.

these tasks. The holding company should also appoint a chief compliance officer to take charge of implementing a groupwide compliance policy, including AML/CFT, data protection issues, customer compliance, greenwashing, and anti-corruption issues. The Internal Audit Unit will need to be upgraded to effectively become a groupwide function. The need to upgrade Baiterek's internal control framework is further elaborated in chapter 6.

Table 4.1 summarizes the chapter's recommendations, highlights responsible entities for implementation, and outlines expected results.

REFERENCE

OECD (Organisation for Economic Co-operation and Development). 2015. *OECD Guidelines on Corporate Governance of State-Owned Enterprises.* 2015 edition. Paris: OECD Publishing. http://dx.doi.org/10.1787/9789264244160-en.

5 Double Bottom Line and Impact Measurement

Financial institutions with a development mandate base their decisions about financing individual investment projects on the double bottom line principle. This chapter reviews the approaches of selected development finance institutions (DFIs) to defining their double bottom line and to measuring and verifying impact. It then describes the approach followed by the World Bank and other international financial institutions (IFIs) and makes specific recommendations for definition of the double bottom line and impact measurement by Baiterek.

APPROACHES FOLLOWED BY SELECTED DEVELOPMENT FINANCE INSTITUTIONS

Global Energy Efficiency and Renewable Energy Fund

The Global Energy Efficiency and Renewable Energy Fund (GEEREF) was established by the European Commission in 2006 and launched in 2008. The initial funding by the European Union, Germany, and Norway totaled €112 million. The fund is a public-private partnership. The European Investment Bank Group, which advises the GEEREF, successfully concluded its fundraising from private sector investors in May 2015, when total funds under management came to €222 million. GEEREF is a fund of funds. It invests in private equity funds that focus on renewable energy and energy efficiency projects in emerging markets. As of mid-2023, GEEREF had invested in 15 funds across Africa, Latin America, and the Caribbean. The fund investment period closed at the end of May 2019 and the fund is now fully invested.

GEEREF investments aim to bring equal benefits for a triple bottom line centered on people, planet, and profit. As part of its focus on people, the fund seeks to provide access to sustainable energy and increase energy efficiency in developing countries and economies in transition. As part of its focus on the planet, the fund seeks to fight climate change and contribute to a sustainable environment. As part of its focus on profit, the fund seeks to achieve robust financial returns. Clean energy infrastructure projects target yields of about 15 percent at the operating level with a view to delivering gross fund returns in the range of 15–25 percent.

FIGURE 5.1
GEEREF impact metrics

Pillar 1: Clean energy	Pillar 2: Environment/climate change
• Installed capacity (MW) • Electricity generated (MWh) • Energy efficiency savings (MWh)	• Net emissions reduced (tons of CO_2 equivalent)
Pillar 3: Sustainable development	**Pillar 4: Financial leverage**
• Beneficiary households • Beneficiary SMEs	• Fund private capital multiplier

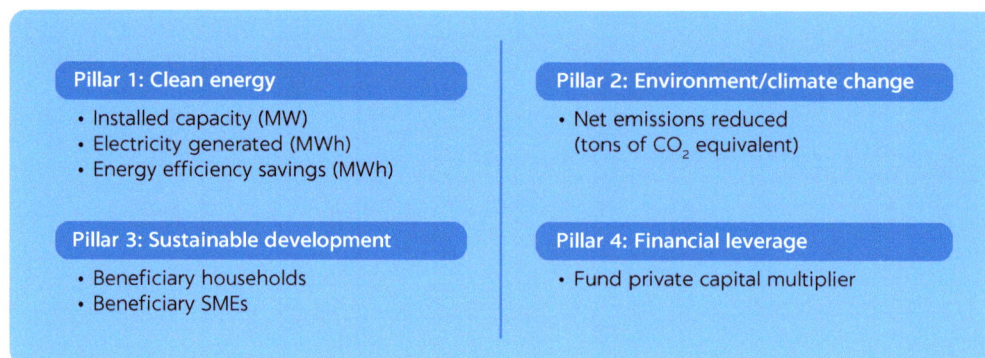

Source: GEEREF 2021.
Note: GEEREF = Global Energy Efficiency and Renewable Energy Fund; MW = megawatts; MWh = megawatt-hours; SMEs = small and medium enterprises.

The fund's impact metrics are articulated around four pillars: clean energy, environment/climate change, sustainable development, and financial leverage (see figure 5.1).

The fund's impact metrics are calculated on a gross basis. That is, impact metrics do not consider whether the capacity would have been installed, or net emissions reduced, or energy savings realized, in the absence of financing by GEEREF. However, the crowding-in effect on private investors is captured through the fund's private capital multiplier.

The fund verifies the impact of its investments through three layers of data. First, it measures actual reported values from the relevant financial year from each of the investments in each portfolio in the reporting period. Second, it measures impact for the current portfolio and the target portfolio. The current portfolio assumes that all projects in the existing portfolio (under development, under construction, and in operation) are fully operational for a full year. The figure provides a snapshot of the expected annual impact of the projects that are in the portfolio once they become operational. The fund also measures impacts for the targeted portfolio. The targeted portfolio assumes that all projects in the current portfolio and in the pipeline are fully operational for a full year. This figure provides a snapshot of the expected annual impact of all the projects that GEEREF will end up supporting. These data are provided across the four pillars. Third, the fund calculates the official development assistance (ODA) impact, which shows the impact achieved by ODA investors that catalyzed the private-investor limited partners. This step calculates the ratio of public to total commitments and derives a final multiplier for all capital invested through GEEREF's portfolio projects relative to the initial ODA commitments to GEEREF.

Asia Climate Partners

Asia Climate Partners (ACP) is a US$450 million hybrid investment fund targeting the renewable energy, resource efficiency, and environmental sectors in emerging Asia. The fund was launched in 2014 as a joint initiative of the Asian Development Bank (ADB), Robeco, and ORIX Corporation. Robeco is an international asset manager domiciled in the Netherlands and fully owned

TABLE 5.1 **ACP impact assessment metrics**

METRIC	DETAILS
Total MW of clean energy installed	By type (on grid, off grid)
	By technology (wind, solar, hydropower, other)
MWh of clean energy generated	By type (on grid, off grid)
	By technology (wind, solar, hydropower, other)
MWh of energy saved	Specific to energy efficiency investments
Tons of carbon dioxide equivalent (CO_2e) avoided	—
Number of households with access to clean energy	By type (household grid connection, dedicated energy access, district heating)
Jobs created	In construction and operation phases
	Males and females
Number of sustainable supply chain and clean technologies supported	Total number of sectors represented in the investment portfolio
Private and public finance leveraged at the fund level	Fund assets under management
Private and public finance leveraged (debt and equity) at the co-investment level	Total amount invested by third parties in ACP portfolio companies
Public and private finance leveraged (debt and equity) at the portfolio company or project level	Total amount invested by third parties in ACP portfolio companies, including debt raised by portfolio companies for specific projects

Source: Divakaran et al. 2022.
Note: ACP = Asia Climate Partners; MW = megawatts; MWh = megawatt-hours.

by ORIX Corporation. In 2022, the capital held by ACP was from ADB (US$100 million), the UK government (US$94.3 million), ORIX Asia Capital (US$100 million), and other investors (US$155.7 million).

ACP aims to demonstrate that it is possible to invest in green finance in Asia on a commercial basis while adhering to rigorous environmental, social, and governance (ESG) standards. The fund selects investment projects based on a double bottom line of financial return and economic impact measurement. The metrics contained in ACP's impact assessment are presented in table 5.1. These metrics are verified yearly and included in the ACP annual report.

Ireland Strategic Investment Fund

The Ireland Strategic Investment Fund (ISIF) was established by the government of Ireland in 2014 with initial capital of €7.6 billion from the National Pensions Reserve Fund. The objective of the fund is to invest on a commercial basis in a manner designed to support economic activity and employment in the country. The fund has a stated target of a 1:2.6 private capital multiplier for its invested capital (see Halland et al. 2016).

The selection of investments by ISIF is subject to a double bottom line based on financial and economic impact criteria. The financial criteria are as follows: First, the investment performance goal is to exceed the average cost of government debt. Second, there are to be no withdrawals from the fund for budgetary purposes before 2025; thereafter a dividend-type payment of up to 4 percent a year may be paid to the exchequer. Third, investments are not to have a negative impact on the net borrowing of the general government for any year.

ISIF measures the economic impact of its investments by applying three principles: additionality, displacement, and deadweight.

- *Additionality* refers to the additional economic benefits to gross value added (GVA) and gross domestic product (GDP) likely to arise from the investment under consideration above what would have taken place in any case. Elements of economic additionality at the project level include GVA, employment creation, and qualitative impacts such as contribution to the country's enabling infrastructure, innovation, and efficiency. Social and environmental impacts are not included in the calculation of additionality, but are covered under ISIF's Sustainability and Responsible Investment Strategy and its adherence to the United Nations Principles for Responsible Investment and the Santiago Principles.
- *Displacement* refers to instances where an investment's additionality is reduced at the overall economy level due to a reduction in economic benefits elsewhere in the economy. For example, an investee company that competes with other domestic companies would reduce the investment's overall impact on GDP.
- *Deadweight* refers to instances where the economic benefits of an investment would have been achieved in the absence of such investment, such as the case of an investee company that would have attracted private capital regardless of ISIF's participation.

Investment opportunities that generate economic additionality, at low levels of displacement and deadweight, are likely to deliver high economic impact at the level of the overall economy over the long term. Economic additionality can come in many forms, including increased output (turnover) and profits (operating surplus, employment, net exports, and capital expenditure). The supply of infrastructure may also create additionality in the future by facilitating future competitiveness of the economy. Similarly, innovation and investment in research and development may generate long-term additionality that is not immediately evident but is necessary for long-term sustainable economic growth. ISIF impact metrics are shown in box 5.1. These metrics are verified by ISIF management and included in the ISIF yearly impact report; all are calculated year-over-year.

BOX 5.1

Ireland Strategic Investment Fund impact metrics

- Jobs supported by ISIF capital
- Gross value added
- Turnover
- Employment by region
- Wage bill
- Exports

Source: NTMA 2021.
Note: All metrics are calculated year-over-year. ISIF = Ireland Strategic Investment Fund.

Banco Nacional de Desenvolvimento (Brazil)

The Banco Nacional de Desenvolvimento (BNDES) publishes disbursements and number of operations by United Nations Sustainable Development Goal (SDG) as part of its annual report. Table 5.2 shows the bank's achievements by SDG in 2021.

Development Bank of South Africa

The Development Bank of South Africa (DBSA) measures its development outcomes in two dimensions. First, a set of development impact indicators is defined and measured for each business line. Second, the direct and indirect contribution of DBSA actions to selected SDGs and to corresponding National Development Plan outcomes are presented. Under the first dimension, outcome (impact) indicators are presented for each business line. Table 5.3 shows the estimated development impact indicators for the infrastructure-financing business line in 2021.

TABLE 5.2 Indicators of BNDES disbursements and operations in Brazil by United Nations SDG, 2021

SDG	DISBURSEMENTS (R$, MILLIONS)	OPERATIONS (NUMBER)
1. No poverty	1,899.7	24,576
2. Zero hunger	8,636.5	62,194
3. Good health and well-being	1,424.0	1,181
4. Quality education	116.3	914
5. Gender equality	2.7	73
6. Clean water and sanitation	458.0	132
7. Affordable and clean energy	15,888.1	501
8. Decent work and economic growth	26,256.2	176,805
9. Industry, innovation, and infrastructure	27,909.6	21,052
10. Reduced inequalities	9,519.1	32,601
11. Sustainable cities and communities	878.1	403
12. Responsible consumption and production	2,068.4	1,734
13. Climate action	5,926.5	879
14. Life below water	293.2	422
15. Life on land	742.2	533
16. Peace, justice, and strong institutions	92.9	55
17. Partnerships for the goals	2,679.3	179

Source: BNDES 2022.
Note: BNDES = Banco Nacional de Desenvolvimento; SDG = Sustainable Development Goal.

TABLE 5.3 Development impact indicators for infrastructure-financing business line in South Africa, 2021

ACTIVITY LINE	DEVELOPMENT OUTCOME INDICATOR	RESULT
Energy	Total households impacted	70,122
Water	Total households impacted	39,945
Rehabilitation of roads	Total households impacted	101,698
Sanitation	Total households impacted	19,876
Anticipated direct construction jobs	Number of jobs created	8,320
Anticipated direct operational jobs	Number of jobs created	2,980

Source: DBSA 2022.

Under the second dimension, DBSA presents the direct and indirect contribution of its actions to the SDGs and to National Development Plan outcomes. In 2021, DBSA actions contributed directly to six SDGs—that is, SDG 6 (clean water and sanitation), SDG 7 (affordable and clean energy), SDG 9 (industry, innovation, and infrastructure), SDG 11 (sustainable cities and communities), SDG 13 (climate action), and SDG 17 (partnerships for the goals).

APPROACH FOLLOWED BY THE WORLD BANK AND OTHER IFIs AND RECOMMENDATIONS FOR BAITEREK

In principle, in choosing which projects to finance, international good practice for the double bottom line approach selects the project design with the highest economic rate of return (ERR) among mutually exclusive alternatives, subject to a hurdle internal rate of return (IRR) (EIB 2013; World Bank 1998). In most cases, IFIs enter the project cycle when project alternatives have already been analyzed and one project alternative has been selected by the government agency concerned. Hence, in most cases, IFIs limit their analysis to estimation of the ERR and the IRR of the selected alternative. In practice, this means that government entities such as Baiterek have the primary responsibility for identifying mutually exclusive project alternatives and for carrying out a thorough ERR and IRR analysis of each project alternative.

The hurdle IRR is the minimum IRR necessary to protect the IFI's capital. As a reference, the International Finance Corporation (IFC) sets its hurdle rate at 8 percent. Baiterek can set its hurdle rate based on the currency in which it manages its balance sheet (tenge) and at the level of project, program, subsidiary, and holding as a percentage that ensures adequate protection of capital.

The ERR is estimated using the cost-benefit analysis methodology, which compares the situation with the project versus without the project. Project benefits and costs are defined in terms of their wider economic impact for the country. For example, positive impacts include increased economic growth, reduced poverty, alleviated income inequality, and mitigated greenhouse gas (GHG) emissions. Project costs are defined in terms of their opportunity cost, that is, the benefit foregone by not using the same resource for the best available alternative investment, as measured by the rate on long-term government bonds. Discounted benefits and costs are valued using shadow prices, which are defined as the increase in welfare resulting from a marginal change in the availability of goods and services or factors of production.

A variety of approaches may be followed to estimate shadow prices in the economic analysis of projects, depending on data available. At the most advanced level, shadow prices may be estimated using a dynamic macroeconomic optimization model—for example, a dynamic computable general equilibrium model that maximizes output over time, subject to input-output production and resource constraints. The dual solution of the model generates a set of shadow prices for each product and resource for every year over the simulation horizon.

Alternatively, in the absence of a macroeconomic optimization model, shadow prices may be estimated individually—using methodologies that adjust market prices to reflect opportunity costs (see World Bank 1998). Shadow prices of outputs and inputs in domestic currency may differ from their market prices due to additional distortions generated by government and private sector market participants. These include distortionary domestic taxes and subsidies or the presence of noncompetitive market structures. They also include externalities that are not internalized by the market, such as GHG emissions or contributions to systemic financial instability. The estimation of shadow prices of non-tradable goods uses a multistage process that includes estimating market distortions, upper and lower bounds for the shadow price of goods, and the opportunity cost of goods based on demand and supply elasticities.

In line with the High-Level Commission on Carbon Prices, the World Bank recommends that a project's economic analysis use a low and a high estimate of the shadow price of carbon. The pricing starts at a low of US$40 and a high of US$80 in 2020, and increases to US$50 and US$100 by 2030. The World Bank also recommends extrapolating the band for the shadow price of carbon from 2030 to 2050 using the same growth rate of 2.25 percent per year that is implicit between 2020 and 2030, leading to values of US$78 and US$156 by 2050. In addition, it recommends using the GHG Protocol Scope 2 methodology for the calculation of the GHG emissions of investment projects.

Inequality concerns should be built into the ERR analysis. As governments in emerging markets face constraints on the use of the fiscal system to efficiently redistribute income, the ERR analysis methodology includes the use of distributional weights that attach a different value to a marginal increase in consumption for various household groups, including households in disadvantaged regions. Box 5.2 outlines the methodological steps for project selection and subsidy determination under double bottom line objectives.

Methodologies for large and small projects supported by DFIs can differ to reflect capacity and resource constraints. Given the significant data and analytics

---

Steps for the double bottom line economic and financial analysis of investment projects

The economic and financial analysis of investment projects under the double bottom line approach follows these steps:

1. Define investment project development objectives and measurable development indicators.
2. Identify mutually exclusive project alternatives. These alternatives may encompass different technologies, project scales, or project locations.
3. For each project alternative, estimate the expected economic rate of return (ERR) of the project, comparing the situation with and without the project.
4. Rank project alternatives in accordance with their expected ERR.
5. Estimate the expected internal rate of return (IRR) of the top project alternative. If the expected IRR is higher than the hurdle rate, accept the alternative.
6. If the expected IRR is lower than the hurdle rate, consider a blended finance package of concessional and commercial finance with the objective of delivering an expected IRR higher than the hurdle rate for commercial investors, and requiring that the subsidy of the concessional finance component be lower than the differential between the ERRs of the top project alternative and the second-best alternative.
7. If the needed subsidy rate of the concessional finance component is higher than the ERR differential between the first-best and the second-best project alternatives, abandon the first-best alternative and apply steps 5 and following with the second-best project alternative.

demands of the ERR cost-benefit methodology, DFIs generally apply the methodology for medium to large projects only. For small projects, the double bottom line can be expressed in terms of the IRR and of the social and environmental impact of the project using the IRIS+ impact measurement and management methodology developed by the Global Investment Impact Network (GIIN). For many small projects under a large program, the ERR cost-benefit methodology can be applied at the level of the program (not the level of the small projects).

For small projects, the World Bank recommends the use of the IRIS+ impact measurement and management methodology, which is based on four pillars:

1. *Setting goals and expectations.* Goals should consider the effects an investment has on people and the planet and should balance investor expectations for risk, return, liquidity, and impact.

2. *Defining strategies.* IRIS+ includes commonly deployed strategic goals that are backed by best practices and evidence. Strategic goals that are most relevant to the impact of investment activities under the project should be selected.

3. *Selecting metrics and setting targets.* IRIS+ core metric sets are the evidence- and best practice–based sets of IRIS+ metrics used to assess the effects of any investment or enterprise across the five dimensions of impact.

4. *Measuring, tracking, and using the data and reporting.* Impact measurement and management considers information about risks, returns, and impacts to learn, adjust, and improve investment decision-making.

The five dimensions of impact are the following:

1. *What:* What *outcome* is the beneficiary enterprise contributing to, and how important are the outcomes to stakeholders?

2. *Who:* Who experiences the outcome effect, and how underserved are they in relation to the targeted outcome?

3. *Contribution:*
   - Beneficiary enterprise (investee): How does the effect compare to and contribute to what would likely occur anyway?
   - Investors: How much do investors contribute to the impact of the underlying investee?

4. *How much:* How much of the outcome effect occurs during the project time period?

5. *Risk:* Which risk factors are significant, and how likely is it that the outcome is different from the one anticipated?

Simpler practical alternatives for impact measurement could use benchmarking project indicators for beneficiaries (enterprises, households) against a control group (industry peers, nonbeneficiary households) using parallel trends in employment, value added, or GHG emissions (energy efficiency). It is important that the underlying basic data entering the impact measurement metrics and their computation are collected or produced through independent statistics—such as by the national statistics bureau.

The quantitative impact verification of projects could be based on quasi-experimental ex post evaluations. These require the collection of comprehensive data on treated groups and control groups of beneficiaries (such as firms) and market participants (such as financial institutions). The impact evaluations could employ techniques such as the difference-in-differences estimations in a regression setup with relevant controls for confounding factors or synthetic control methodology. It is important not only that Baiterek projects (support programs) be exposed to independent impact evaluations, but that Baiterek publish data for other independent (third-party) entities so they can conduct such impact evaluations and scrutinize Baiterek operations and their impact on their own.

Figure 5.2 summarizes the data inputs, computations, and indicators used at the investment selection stage, the investment monitoring stage, and the investment impact evaluation stage. Basically, at the investment project selection stage the decision-makers need the calculations of ERR and IRR for all investment project alternatives, using the assumptions about key performance indicators (KPIs) as inputs. For the investment monitoring stage, key monitoring indicators need to be developed based on the KPIs for the investment project beneficiaries and the counterfactual—for example, jobs at beneficiary small and medium enterprises (SMEs) versus jobs at matching nonbeneficiary SMEs. At the impact evaluation stage, a rigorous impact evaluation using difference-in-differences estimations focused on KPIs as outcome variables needs to be carried out for matching treated and nontreated beneficiaries (such as SMEs).

The third-party impact assessment can be done annually by the Auditor General Office (AGO) in conjunction with deeper periodic evaluations of long-term development impact conducted either by AGO or by the Agency for Strategic Planning and Reforms (ASPIR). Assessing compliance with development goals is beyond the mandate of the supervisor (the Agency for Regulation and Development of the Financial Markets [AFR]); however, AFR can still play an active role in ensuring that the holding company is actively assessing the climate and environmental risks (or, more broadly, the ESG risks). The third-party oversight and verification of impact can be done by the AGO, which will have to either build the needed

FIGURE 5.2

Data inputs, measurement methodologies, and indicators at the investment selection, monitoring, and evaluation stages

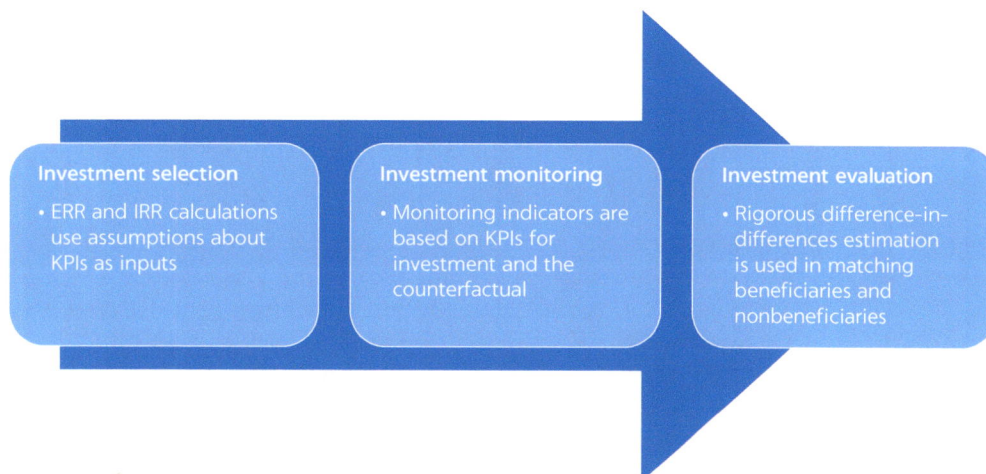

Source: World Bank.
Note: ERR = economic rate of return; IRR = internal rate of return; KPI = key performance indicator.

TABLE 5.4 Recommendations: Double bottom line and impact measurement

ACTION (FOR SUBSIDIARIES WITH DEVELOPMENT MANDATE)	RESPONSIBLE ENTITY	EXPECTED RESULT
For large investment projects, select projects based on maximization of ERR among mutually exclusive project alternatives, subject to a minimum IRR (hurdle rate)	Baiterek Board	Ensure alignment of investment projects financed by subsidiaries with development mandates with country's environmental and social objectives, including the Nationally Determined Contribution under the Paris Agreement
Estimate the ERR using the methodology of the World Bank (and other multilateral development banks) for economic analysis of projects, which is based on shadow prices, including the shadow price of carbon	Baiterek Board	Same as above
For small investment projects, select projects based on the maximization of economic and social impact using GIIN's IRIS+ impact measurement methodology; and/or make selection based on ERR at the level of the investment program (rather than project)	Baiterek Board	Same as above
For all projects, calculate GHG emissions based on GHG Protocol Scope 2 (at a minimum)	Baiterek Board	Same as above

Source: World Bank.
Note: ERR = economic rate of return; GHG = greenhouse gas; GIIN = Global Impact Investment Network; IRR = internal rate of return.

capacity or outsource independent annual impact verification—to local financial auditors, credit rating agencies (which themselves may need to build up capacity and skills), or existing specialized impact verification companies globally. The Parliamentary Committee on Finance and Economics should continue discussing the results of AGO verification with Baiterek's Impact Committee to improve the methodology, measurement, and integrity of its impact measurement framework.[1] When periodic impact evaluations are completed, the AGO will inform the Impact Committee to improve the methodology, measurement, and integrity of its impact measurement framework. Another policy option is to assign the periodic evaluations of Baiterek's impact to ASPIR in accordance with its mandate for monitoring impact of reforms. Table 5.4 summarizes the recommendations for Baiterek as it transitions toward proper double bottom line management and impact measurement practices.

NOTE

1. One of ASPIR's mandates is the assessment of long-term development impacts, and the agency is less exposed than government ministries to the political cycle.

REFERENCES

BNDES (Banco Nacional de Desenvolvimento). 2022. *BNDES Integrated Annual Report 2021.* Rio de Janeiro: BNDES. https://web.bndes.gov.br/bib/jspui/bitstream/1408/22504/1 /PRPer161100_Relat%C3%B3rio%20anual%20BNDES_2021_eng.pdf.

DBSA (Development Bank of South Africa). 2022. *DBSA Integrated Annual Report 2021.* Midrand, South Africa: DBSA.

Divakaran, Shanthi, Håvard Halland, Gianni Lorenzato, Paul Rose, and Sebastian Sarmiento-Saher. 2022. *Strategic Investment Funds: Establishment and Operations.* International Development in Focus. Washington, DC: World Bank. https://openknowledge.worldbank .org/handle/10986/37557.

EIB (European Investment Bank). 2013. *The Economic Appraisal of Investment Projects at the EIB*. Luxembourg: EIB.

GEEREF (Global Energy Efficiency and Renewable Energy Fund). 2021. "Global Energy Efficiency and Renewable Energy Fund Impact Report 2021: A Catalyst for Clean Power." https://geeref.com/assets/documents/2021%20GEEREF%20Impact%20Report.pdf.

Halland, Håvard, Michael Noel, Silvana Tordo, and Jacob J. Kloper-Owens. 2016. "Strategic Investment Funds: Opportunities and Challenges." Policy Research Working Paper 7851, World Bank, Washington, DC. http://hdl.handle.net/10986/25168.

NTMA (National Treasury Management Agency). 2021. "Ireland Strategic Investment Fund: H1 2021 Update Incorporating Economic Impact Report FY 2020." https://isif.ie/uploads/publications/070921H120201-Performance-and-FY2020-update-published3102022.pdf.

World Bank. 1998. *Handbook on Economic Analysis of Investment Operations*. Washington, DC: World Bank.

6 Structure and Governance of the Holding Company's Subsidiaries

INTRODUCTION

There is scope for substantial consolidation of the subsidiary structure to improve the governance of Baiterek and its subsidiaries—even though the corporate structure of Baiterek Holding has been streamlined from 11 subsidiaries to 8 in recent years. Currently, the legal entity structure is organized mainly through business activities/models that mix three areas of focus in a rather unorganized manner: (i) sectoral specialization—entrepreneurship, exports, housing, agriculture, infrastructure; (ii) financial instruments—equity/quasi-equity financing, credit lines/debt/leasing, credit guarantees, and interest rate subsidies; and (iii) wholesale versus direct market participation and competition with private financial firms.

The World Bank recommends considering a new subsidiary structure along impact management principles that suggest three subsidiary groupings under Baiterek, managed on the basis of their objectives (figure 6.1).

- The *Commercialization and Privatization Group* (CPG) will group Tier 2 institutions with commercial mandates that are operating in the market and competing with private financial institutions, and that will sooner or later be privatized—such as Sberbank, KazAgroFinance, most of Otbasy, and part of Agrarian Credit Corporation (ACC). This group will include future national-ized banks if needed. CPG institutions will be registered as financial institu-tion(s) and supervised by the Agency for Regulation and Development of the Financial Markets (AFR).
- The *Strategic Finance Group* (SFG) will group Tier 1 institutions with a double bottom line—that is, a minimum internal rate of return (IRR) to protect capital and development mandates in terms of economic rate of return (ERR) for greenhouse gas emissions reduction, jobs creation, and revenue generation impacts. The SFG institution will include the Development Bank of Kazakhstan (DBK), Entrepreneurship Development Fund (DAMU), Qazaqstan Investment Corporation (QIC), and ACC and Kazakhstan Housing Company (KHC) Tier 1 (wholesale) operations. One of the SFG objectives and targeted impacts will be market creation and private capital mobilization. SFG institutions will be registered as financial institutions and supervised by AFR.

FIGURE 6.1

Proposed subsidiary structure for Baiterek

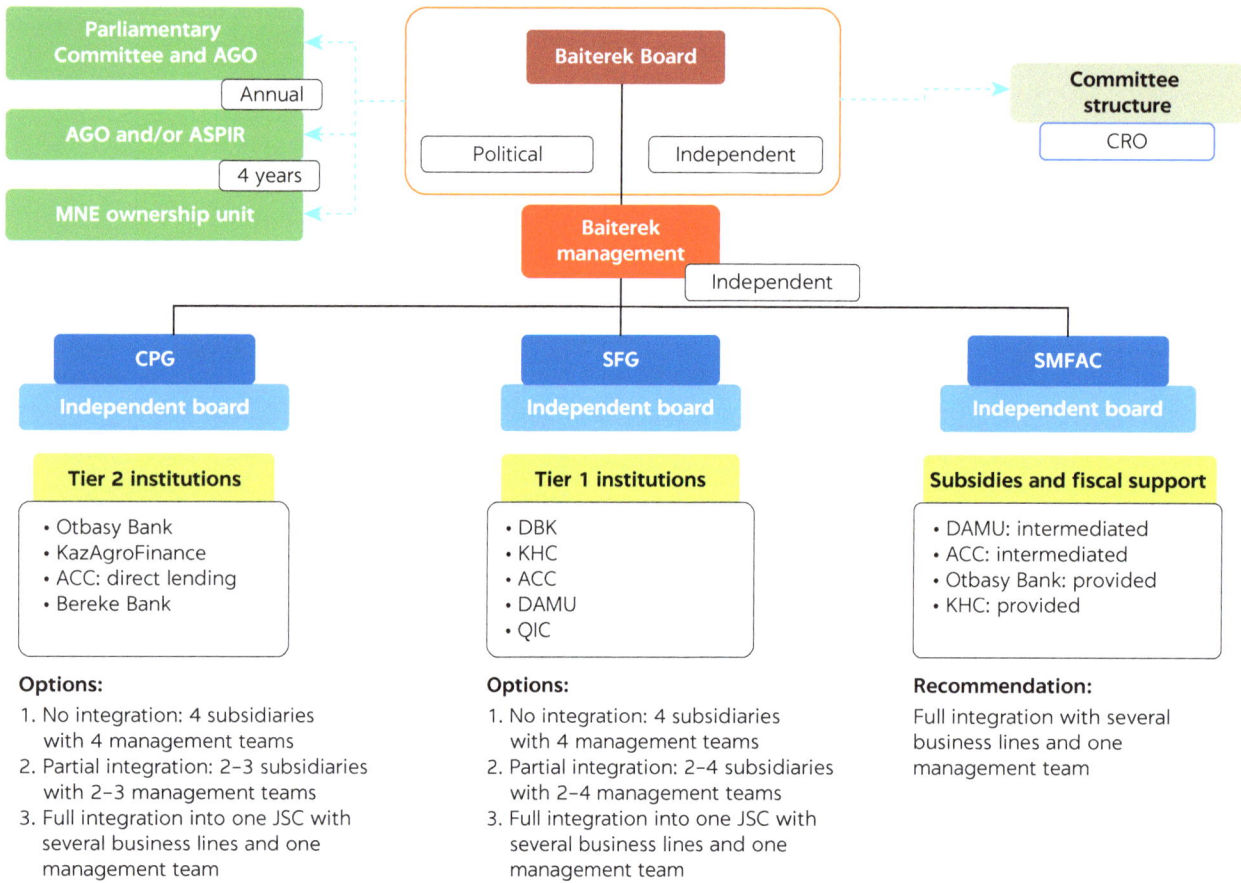

Source: World Bank.

Note: ACC = Agrarian Credit Corporation; AGO = Auditor General Office; ASPIR = Agency for Strategic Planning and Reforms; CPG = Commercialization and Privatization Group; CRO = chief risk officer; DAMU = Entrepreneurship Development Fund; DBK = Development Bank of Kazakhstan; KHC = Kazakhstan Housing Company; MNE = Ministry of National Economy; QIC = Qazaqstan Investment Corporation; SFG = Strategic Finance Group; SMFAC = Subsidy Management and Fiscal Agent Corporation.

• The *Subsidy Management and Fiscal Agent Corporation JSC* (SMFAC) will consolidate subsidy design and implementation (targeting mechanisms, sunset clauses, and their triggers) and fiscal agent operations as a fee business for Baiterek, with a possible contribution from donors. Examples of business lines to be consolidated under the SMFAC grouping include interest rate subsidies offered by DAMU and ACC (and its subsidiary KazAgroFinance) and financed by the Ministry of Finance/Ministry of National Economy and Ministry of Agriculture.

This transformation can be programmatic because effective implementation of this recommendation will have substantial legal and financial implications. It will involve several demergers and mergers that will need to be based on carve-out processes. The complexity of this reform will be considerable, but so will the returns anticipated upon its completion. The first step should be commissioning a legal firm to prepare a feasibility study and roadmap for the restructuring. The programmatic implementation could start by forming common boards for similar business lines and allowing the boards to decide on the pace of integrating subsidiaries or business lines within each group. In this structure, the subsidiaries within each group maintain their separate legal corporate structure, but the boards of the subsidiaries within each group are composed of the same directors, who effectively constitute the common board of the group.

Figure 6.1 summarizes the recommended governance and subsidiary structure to guide reform of Baiterek. For example, based on the decisions of its board of directors, the CPG group could (i) group just the relevant commercially oriented business lines of Tier 2 institutions (no corporate integration), (ii) partially integrate the business (immediately or over time), or (iii) fully integrate all the businesses in one corporate (JSC) entity. The future board of directors for the SFG could choose from analogous options of no, partial, or full integration. For SMFAC, full integration of all subsidy intermediation functions and fiscal agent functions in one entity is recommended.

For example, DAMU, with its guarantee programs and credit lines (priced close to the market), would fall under SFG. But the interest subsidy programs that DAMU administers would fall under SMFAC. Alternatively, KazAgroFinance and Otbasy's Tier 2 businesses could fall under CPG as institutions, and any interest and down-payment subsidies they provide would fall under SMFAC. The main objective is to create a clean line for private investors and international financial institutions with different purposes (privatization deals, double bottom line investments) to engage. A complete mapping of current subsidiaries and programs into the three-group structure can be conducted as a follow-up to this report if this recommendation for a rationalized subsidiary structure is adopted for implementation. The groups' boards will be responsible for assessing the potential for mergers within each group and commissioning legal feasibility studies for that purpose.

One motivation for this three-group structure is the consideration given to private capital mobilization. Private capital will shy away from entering privatization deals of public commercial entities if these entail a government mandate for socioeconomic impacts that cannot be monetized and need to be subsidized. Similarly, private debt and equity investors are likely to shy away from subsidiary structures that include budget subsidies, which the government may later force the entity to take over without commensurate funding. It is a government strategy to lower direct subsidies over time, replace them with indirect support such as guarantees, or phase out those that are not needed. CPG and SFG could explicitly target private capital multipliers following the example of the Global Energy Efficiency and Renewable Energy Fund (see chapter 5).

COMMERCIALIZATION AND PRIVATIZATION GROUP GOVERNANCE

The common board of directors of CPG will be composed of five to seven independent directors. All directors will have expertise and experience in the holding and privatization of state-owned financial institutions. The external directors will be recruited based on an open international competition managed by a reputable international private recruitment company. The "fit, proper, and independence" test of the external directors will be executed by a reputable international private integrity due diligence (IDD) company. External directors will be appointed for a term of five years, renewable once.

The responsibilities of the common board of directors of CPG will include the following:

- Approve the business and privatization plans of CPG companies and submit them to the Baiterek Board for approval. Privatization would be based on an international competitive process open to private financial institutions domiciled in advanced countries, without direct or indirect participation from the state. The beneficial owners, directors, and managers of candidate financial institutions would be subject to a fit, proper, and independence test administered by a private IDD company.
- Approve the semiannual activity reports of CPG companies and submit them to the Baiterek Board for approval.
- Approve privatization transactions of individual CPG companies in accordance with the business and privatization plans approved by the Baiterek Board.
- Approve CPG companies' annual reports.

The common board of directors of the CPG will establish specialized common board committees with the following responsibilities:

- The *Market Impact/Creation and Privatization Committee* will be responsible for monitoring CPG impact on financial market development and private capital activation; developing sunset clauses for exiting a market segment to avoid crowding out private capital; and requesting assessment of privatization readiness of CPG companies, including assessments of the potential investor landscape.
- The *Risk Committee* will keep the board informed about integrated risk management across the group and about types of risks (financial, enterprise, and impact-related) with the help of the chief risk officer. The Risk Committee will include functions of a compliance committee that will be responsible for conflict of interest, anti-corruption, and AML/CFT (anti–money laundering and combating the financing of terrorism) policies and procedures, and for overseeing the execution of all on-site and off-site supervision requirements from AFR. It will be also responsible for approving the environmental and social management system (ESMS) of the subsidiary groups and companies consistent with the ESMS of the holding company.
- The *Audit Committee* will be responsible for overseeing the internal audit function and for organizing the annual external audit of CPG companies.
- The *Remuneration and Compensation Committee* will be responsible for establishing the human resources policies and procedures of CPG companies.

The management boards of CPG companies will be composed solely of independent senior experts with experience in the holding and privatization of state-owned financial institutions. Management board members will be recruited through an open international competition carried out by a reputable international private recruitment company. Selected candidates will be subject to a fit, proper, and independence test carried out by a reputable international IDD company. Management board members will be recruited for a term of four years, renewable once—preferably based on successful completion of a well-designed performance contract.

The responsibilities of the management boards will be as follows:

- Review the business, commercialization, and privatization plans prepared by CPG companies and submit them to the CPG Board of Directors for approval.
- Review the semiannual activity reports prepared by CPG companies and submit them to the CPG Board of Directors for approval.
- Structure privatization transactions of CPG companies with international private strategic investors, submit them to the CPG Board of Directors for approval, and execute them.
- Process the capital contributions from the holding company to CPG companies and the dividends and privatization proceeds payments from CPG companies, and submit them to the CPG Board of Directors for approval.
- Fulfill all on-site and off-site supervision requirements of the AFR under the oversight of the CPG Risk Committee.
- Execute all conflict of interest, anti-corruption, and AML/CFT measures as directed by the Risk Committee, including mitigating greenwashing risks at the corporate, market intermediary, and beneficiary levels.
- Prepare CPG companies' ESMSs in accordance with the holding company's ESMS and submit them to the CPG Risk Committee for approval.
- Prepare CPG companies' impact measurement assessments covering beneficiaries and markets—respecting competitive neutrality principles—and impact risks (just-transition, green bubble creation).
- Prepare CPG companies' annual reports and submit them to the CPG Board of Directors for approval.

The independent Internal Audit Unit of the CPG will report directly to the Audit Committee. The Chief Risk Office Unit will report to the CEO and/or the board's integrated Risk Committee on financial, enterprise, and impact-related risks.

STRATEGIC FINANCE GROUP GOVERNANCE

The governance structure of SFG will be similar to that of the CPG, but with the following differences:

- The five to seven external directors will have expertise and experience in managing state-owned financial institutions with a development mandate and in providing guidance on meeting the double bottom line of maximizing development impact and market creation while achieving a minimum financial return to protect capital.
- The board of directors will approve the development plans and the semiannual activity reports submitted by SFG companies. The development plans and semiannual activity reports will be based on the double bottom line (as explained previously) and will not include privatization plans.
- The Impact Committee will be responsible for approving the impact framework of SFG and keeping the board advised of advances in impact framework formulations, including contribution, attribution, measurement, and verification—especially across socioeconomic and green dimensions of impact. In addition, the Impact Committee will separately focus on market creation and private capital mobilization at the fund/bank/company level as well as the project level—including participation in syndications and other risk pooling financial structures.

- The board will approve the capital contributions from the holding company to SFG companies and the dividends and exit proceeds payments from the subsidiaries to SFC. Exit proceeds will consist of exits and liquidations of hybrid investment funds invested by QIC. There will be no privatization proceeds.
- The management board will not execute any privatization transactions.

SUBSIDY MANAGEMENT AND FISCAL AGENT CORPORATION GOVERNANCE

The governance structure of SMFAC will be similar to the governance structure of the CPG and SFG, with the following differences:

- The SMFAC will not be regulated by the AFR.
- The three to five professional directors will have expertise and experience in designing and managing government subsidies, in particular through state-owned financial institutions, as well as in providing guidance on the development impact of subsidy structures, including proper targeting that also seeks to minimize market distortions. Additional expertise on fiscal agency functions (and subnational financing) can be considered before this function is removed from Baiterek's purview (as recommended).
- The board of directors will be responsible for approving the subsidy policy of SMFAC in accordance with the mandate defined by the Ministry of National Economy, the Baiterek Board, and responsible ministries in a cycle of the medium-term expenditure framework in which expenditures on subsidies will be programmed.
- The Impact Committee will be responsible for approving the impact framework, including contribution, attribution, measurement, and verification—especially across socioeconomic and green dimensions of impact.
- The board of directors will be responsible for approving SMFAC's annual activity reports.
- The board of directors will be responsible for approving the SMFAC's annual report.
- The Risk (Compliance) Committee will not be responsible for on-site and off-site supervisory actions by AFR.
- The management board will be composed of senior experts with experience in designing and managing government subsidies in financial services, in particular through state-owned financial institutions, as well as in ensuring maximum development impact through proper targeting and mitigation of market distortions.
- The management board will be responsible for managing the subsidies to qualified firms and households—including through market intermediaries—based on the subsidy policy approved by the board of directors.
- The management board will be responsible for preparing SMFAC's annual report and submitting it to the board of directors for approval.

Table 6.1 summarizes the recommendations, responsible entities, and expected results for reforming Baiterek's subsidiary structure to better manage for impact.

TABLE 6.1 **Recommendations: Baiterek subsidiaries' structure and governance**

ACTION	RESPONSIBLE ENTITY	EXPECTED RESULT
Establish three subsidiary groups • Commercialization and Privatization Group • Strategic Finance Group • Subsidy Management and Fiscal Agent Corporation	Baiterek Board	Alignment of subsidiaries' structure and management with their objectives
Establish a common board for each subsidiary group	Baiterek Board	Focus of board and management expertise on particular group objectives (commercial, double bottom line, subsidy)
Compose subsidiary group and corporation boards solely of independent directors	Baiterek Board	Political independence of subsidiaries' boards and management
Conduct "fit, proper, and independence" tests of subsidiary board members through private international IDD company	Baiterek Board	Integrity of subsidiaries' management

Source: World Bank.
Note: IDD = integrity due diligence.

7 Risk Management Structure and Mechanisms

Baiterek is a public holding company that owns a collection of financial businesses with different development objectives. It currently operates as a diversified financial holding company, with a collection of financial businesses that have little, if any, integration across them. Some of them are purely retail or commercial banking businesses (for example, housing finance, agribusiness), whereas others are linked to corporate finance activities or other combined initiatives within the entities of Baiterek.[1] Every single subsidiary has its own finance, operations, and information technology capabilities, whereas the role of Baiterek, as the parent holding company, is ensuring centralized strategic direction, the harmonization of minimum internal control and risk management standards, and effective oversight of the subsidiaries' management.[2] See Baiterek (2022) for more details.

Nonetheless, the risk management model for Baiterek subsidiaries combines a centralized and decentralized approach. As has been explained previously (chapter 3), the management model of the group is essentially mixed. Management of the Development Bank of Kazakhstan (DBK) appears to be highly centralized and dependent on the parent company, whereas the lines of housing finance (Otbasy), agri-finance (Agrarian Credit Corporation [ACC] and KazAgroFinance), and entrepreneur/export finance (essentially, the Entrepreneurship Development Fund [DAMU]) are heavily decentralized and autonomous. The main subsidiaries/business lines of Baiterek are detailed below:

- *Otbasy* is a second-tier bank that provides housing finance to individuals, with a very large market share; it also manages the housing finance system in the country, encouraging long-term saving to promote access to finance. As of 2023, Otbasy ranks fourth among banks in Kazakhstan based on the amount of equity held. It is largely self-sufficient in terms of liquidity (directly funded through client deposits), risk management, and product development. The bank is managed with very high levels of capital and liquidity and very low leverage, which favors its stability. Concentration risk is negligible, as its clients are in the retail sector. However, concentrated exposure to the housing sector and the property market could be a risk (Otbasy Bank 2022).

- The *Agrarian Credit Corporation* and its direct subsidiary KazAgroFinance engage in agriculture financing, both through direct channels and through second-tier banks, microfinance institutions, leasing companies, and credit partnerships. The business depends heavily on funding from Baiterek, which regularly sends funding downstream as capital increases, and from the national budget.[3] The business is exposed to credit risk, financial risk, and nonfinancial risk (operational, reputational, and so on). ACC operates with high levels of capital and liquidity. Profitability and asset quality are also generally sound, although the subgroup's profitability largely benefits from cheap funding sent downstream by Baiterek. Sectoral risk concentration in agriculture could be an issue, as could operational risk from the local branch network (according to anecdotal reporting of the markets). For more information, see ACC (2022).

- The *Development Bank of Kazakhstan* is tasked with developing the manufacturing industry and infrastructure of Kazakhstan. To this end, it funds large projects across many sectors. DBK receives funds from Baiterek and other state sources and has significant interlinkages with the parent holding company. The most relevant link arises from the credit underwriting policy, which requires that any loan in excess of T 700 billion be approved by DBK's Board of Directors, currently made up of six members. This threshold requires the board to approve most transactions. Even though two board members are independent, the current chair is also a member of Baiterek's Board. This fact may suggest Baiterek's close control and influence over DBK's most relevant credit risk decisions. Although DBK's credit risk underwriting and monitoring practices have not been thoroughly reviewed, they seem to be in line with those of other development banks with regard to know-your-customer, credit risk assessment, and the technical review of the credit risk underwriting process.[4] For more information, see DBK (2022).

- *DAMU* is a fund used to provide loan subsidies, conditional placements of funds (credit lines), and partial credit guarantees for loans to small businesses and entrepreneurs, using the distribution channels of second-tier banks and microfinance institutions (indirect lending). DAMU is entirely dependent on national budget and Baiterek funding. Its main risk is credit risk, which arises in part in relation to the intermediate financial organizations it uses to channel its funds. Furthermore, it is exposed to other financial and nonfinancial risks. DAMU's management model implemented by Baiterek is largely decentralized, which is consistent with the small size of the loans provided by DAMU and the mainly retail nature of its clients. For more information, see DAMU (2022).

Clarifying Baiterek's role in the risk management of this collection of essentially unrelated financial businesses remains a key issue. Consistent with the proposals on corporate governance (outlined in chapter 6), the role of Baiterek in risk management should be based on the holding company's oversight/supervision of the activities of the group. The oversight role of Baiterek's risk management framework will be reflected in the activities it should perform—such as setting the group's risk appetite and risk management standards on a corporate level (including standards for environmental, social, and governance risks) and overseeing the evolution of the risks at a consolidated level (in part by effectively reporting on them to the board Risk Committee).

Risks should be managed at the subsidiary level, while Baiterek's role should be related to oversight, following the three lines of defense (3LoD) model.[5] Each material subsidiary/business line should have its own risk management, compliance monitoring, and internal audit unit (internal control units), which should primarily report to the CEO and/or board of the subsidiary. At the same time, the heads of the subsidiaries' internal control functions, including the internal audit function, should have a double reporting line—hierarchically to their companies' boards and functionally to the relevant head of internal control functions of Baiterek.[6]

The decentralized risk management model combined with consolidated oversight by Baiterek better suits the nature of the group's activities and can hedge the group against political influence. First, the scope, nature, and extent of the activities of Baiterek's subsidiaries are diverse, and the risks are usually unique and mainly limited to one legal entity. Second, the integration among Baiterek's subsidiaries is limited (except for the ACC subgroup). Finally, the risk management autonomy of the subsidiaries can effectively hedge them against undue political influence in their risk decisions, which is particularly relevant for the financing of large projects through DBK. The combination of groupwide internal governance and risk management on the one hand and subsidiary-level governance and internal control functions on the other is well known in banking groups, particularly for those groups that are organized through a parent holding company. This is a very common structure for large South African diversified banking groups (such as Nedbank, Absa, Standard Bank, and FirstRand), British banking groups (such as HSBC, Standard Chartered, and others), and Irish banks.[7] In these cases, the parent oversight role is combined with operational risk management at the subsidiary level. Moreover, international standard setters have clarified group-level internal governance and risk management; see BCBS (2015) and EBA (2021).

The oversight entailed in the risk management function can be articulated over several principles. The principles cover risk management, compliance monitoring, and the internal audit function. First, Baiterek's risk management function should continue to issue corporate policies for risk management that the subsidiaries should adapt to the characteristics of their businesses and follow. Second, it should continue to gather risk data from subsidiaries to define, calculate, and report consolidated risk indicators, perform risk assessments, draw risk maps, and identify the emerging risks on a consolidated basis. Baiterek's risk management function should continue to coordinate and prepare the holding company's consolidated risk appetite and strategy, as well as ensure the prompt reporting of the indicators to Baiterek's corporate bodies—while communicating and requesting changes in cases where breaches are triggered by subsidiaries. Finally, Baiterek's risk management should have sufficient resources to effectively and credibly challenge the risk exposure and risk profile of subsidiaries.

The influence of Baiterek in DBK's credit risk underwriting should not be underestimated. Examining Baiterek's role in defining the group risk management system may wrongly suggest that Baiterek's function is merely to provide strategic direction and oversight. More than 50 percent of the group's credit exposure is assumed through DBK, and as highlighted in the previous paragraphs, the underwriting of any large transaction should be explicitly approved by DBK's Board of Directors, currently chaired by a Baiterek-appointed individual, who also happens to be a member of Baiterek's Board. The combination of these roles (dual hatting) raises questions about the reality of the decentralized risk management model, as a significant share of the credit risk transactions may, in effect, be approved centrally. Actual risk management practices may subject the key credit risk decisions to political interference and conflicts of interest. The most straightforward way to mitigate this possibility is by setting a full independent board of directors at the level of DBK. These changes may also be in line with the 2022 reform of DBK that sought to restructure its activities,[8] and they could serve to more closely link DBK's mission and the financed projects.[9]

The internal audit function of Baiterek should be upgraded. The role of the internal audit function in Baiterek is currently limited in scope and operation. To become an effective corporate internal audit function, it should widen the scope of its activities to exert oversight over all the activities of the Baiterek Group, particularly those undertaken by the subsidiaries. Internal audit should have unrestricted access to all the information and activities across the group, prepare corporate methodologies, engage in groupwide audit planning, and be able to issue recommendations to the group entities. To effectively become a truly corporate function, it should establish groupwide committees to facilitate coordination with the local units. To this end, a functional reporting line should be established between subsidiaries' internal audit units and the Baiterek internal audit function, over and above the hierarchical dependence that the local units have on their respective board audit committees. Importantly, this new oversight corporate model is not expected to result in material overlaps because the local units will continue to be responsible for conducting the internal auditing work in accordance with their corporate mandate. The absence of a groupwide internal audit function may be undermining Baiterek's oversight role, thus bringing into question the application of the 3LoD model at the group level.[10]

A compliance monitoring function should be set up at the Baiterek level to effectively oversee group compliance with laws, regulations, internal codes, and so forth. To this end, the compliance monitoring function will be responsible for ensuring that the activities of the group are carried out in accordance with the applicable legal and ethical standards. Among others, these oversight functions will include establishing groupwide corporate policies and mechanisms for whistleblowing, supervision of the code of conduct's application, data protection, customer compliance, and application of sustainability regulations to avoid greenwashing.

The Baiterek corporate risk management function should continue to be developed around the current approach. Baiterek's risk management function should have a key role in defining the consolidated risk appetite and corporate risk management policies to ensure that Baiterek can enforce consolidated oversight of the groups' risk management. Moreover, the chief risk officer should report directly to the Risk Committee of Baiterek's Board.

Table 7.1 outlines the detailed recommendations on Baiterek's risk management structure and mechanisms.

TABLE 7.1 **Recommendations: Risk management structure and mechanisms**

ACTION	RESPONSIBLE ENTITY	EXPECTED RESULT
Strengthen the risk management function at the Baiterek level, to ensure it has sufficient resources, stature, and expertise to undertake groupwide oversight responsibilities	Baiterek	Increase in risk management capabilities at the Baiterek level
		Reinforcement of corporate risk model
Upgrade Baiterek's internal audit function to a fully fledged group function, in part by amending its stature, reporting lines, and resources	Baiterek	Improvement in the internal control framework for Baiterek at the consolidated level
Create compliance monitoring units at Baiterek and its subsidiaries that partly replace the current internal control functions	Baiterek	Increase in the relevance of and control over compliance monitoring issues, including anti-corruption, greenwashing, AML/CFT, and data protection
Ensure that credit risk underwriting decisions are made at the DBK level and are free of political influence	Baiterek, DBK	Sounder credit risk underwriting standards, more free of conflicts of interests

Source: World Bank.
Note: AML/CFT = anti–money laundering and combating the financing of terrorism; DBK = Development Bank of Kazakhstan.

NOTES

1. Regarding businesses linked to corporate finance activities, a limited synergy or integration may be developed in the future if the Agrarian Credit Corporation (ACC) decides to develop its credit-sharing agreements with second-tier banks or microfinance institutions; this step is called for in the ACC 2020–2023 Strategic Plan. ACC may explore synergies with the Entrepreneurship Development Fund (DAMU), which has experience with these types of indirect credit arrangements. This combined initiative may be particularly relevant against the backdrop of the increasing distribution of ACC's products through third-party channels.

2. Baiterek also develops other functions: for example, treasury management at the group level (including an intragroup lending framework, the provision of guarantees for funding of some of the subsidiaries, currency risk exposure control, and the implementation of consolidated limits for the exposures of Baiterek's subsidiaries to second-tier banks).

3. Although ACC has been raising bonds in the market, and one of its objectives is to reduce its reliance on public funding sources, the prospect of becoming financially self-sufficient seems rather distant.

4. Moreover, DBK's asset quality has remained at relatively low levels: nonperforming loans were at 2.75 percent as of June 2022. Quality is significantly below the very high levels experienced after the onset of the global financial crisis. The nonperforming loan ratio crept up after the COVID-19 pandemic (1.7 percent at end-2019), but it is still at sound levels.

5. The 3LoD model has already been implemented in some subsidiaries and in the parent company.

6. The risk management units may have such a double reporting line currently (the situation is unclear), but the internal audit function does not.

7. More details on the type of structure discussed here can be found in banks' annual reporting; see for example Absa Group Limited (2023), FirstRand (2023), HSBC (2023), Nedbank Group (2023), and SBG (2023).

8. Along with other factors, an action plan approved by the government in January 2022 may have triggered material changes in DBK's strategic development, including (i) a bank cofunding of DBK's public-private partnerships; (ii) the exclusion of funding for projects and operations in the quasi-public sector; (iii) the reduction of DBK's participation in financing tourism, sports and recreation, and hotel sectors as well as communications and telecommunications; (iv) a gradual decline in interbank lending operations; and (v) a requirement to increase transparency for the funded projects.

9. Anecdotal evidence points to inconsistencies between the mission of DBK and the types of projects that are being funded. DBK's mission (as stated on its website, https://www.kdb .kz/en/bank/about-us/) is "to promote the sustainable development of the national economy by investments into the non-resource sector of the country"—but a nonnegligible share of the loan portfolio is invested in the mining sector (15.7 percent as of June 2022, according to data provided by DBK).

10. Although the limited scope and resources of Baiterek's internal audit function might be explained by a desire to avoid the duplication of resources, a broad scope for the internal audit is key for ensuring the credibility of DBK's oversight function across the activities of the group. The same wish to avoid duplication of functions could also explain the risk management function at the Baiterek level.

REFERENCES

Absa Group Limited (2023). "Integrated Report 2022." https://www.absa.africa/wp-content /uploads/2023/03/2022-Absa-Group-Limited-Integrated-Report.pdf.

ACC (Agrarian Credit Corporation). 2022. "Agrarian Credit Corporation Joint Stock Company: Financial Statements for 2021." https://agrocredit.kz/upload/iblock/199/t87 epihu8yxu3symfdht2uw4ey5ecyx0.pdf.

Baiterek. 2022. "Annual Report 2021: Towards Synergy." https://baiterek.gov.kz/upload /iblock/034/flefgaupii69pi38pa6x50xpp7ae7fqo/Baiterek_AR_2021_EN_int.pdf.

BCBS (Basel Committee on Banking Supervision). 2015. "Guidelines: Corporate Governance Principles for Banks." https://Www.Bis.Org/Bcbs/Publ/D328.Pdf.

DAMU (Entrepreneurship Development Fund). 2022. "Annual Report of DAMU Entrepreneurship Development Fund DAMU Joint Stock Company." https://damu.kz /upload/iblock/fc1/1480h8h30fcmip7vu5imt3cohs4pcq7e/%D0%93%D0%9E %D0%94%D0%9E%D0%92%D0%9E%D0%99%20%D0%9E%D0%A2%D0 %A7%D0%95%D0%A2%202021%20(%D0%B0%D0%BD%D0%B3%D0%BB).pdf.

DBK (Development Bank of Kazakhstan). 2022. "Annual Report for the Development Bank of Kazakhstan JSC 2021." https://www.kdb.kz/en/investors/financial-and-annual -reporting/.

EBA (European Banking Authority). 2021. "Final Report on Guidelines on Internal Governance under Directive 2013/36/EU (EBA/GL/2021/05)". July 2, 2021. https://www.eba.europa.eu /sites/default/documents/files/document_library/Publications/Guidelines/2021/1016721 /Final%20report%20on%20Guidelines%20on%20internal%20governance%20under%20 CRD.pdf.

FirstRand. 2023. "2022 Integrated Report." https://www.firstrand.co.za/media/investors /annual-reporting/firstrand-annual-integrated-report-2022.pdf.

HSBC. 2023. "Annual Report and Accounts 2022." https://www.hsbc.com/investors /results-and-announcements/annual-report.

Nedbank Group. 2023. "Pillar 3 Risk and Capital Management Report for the Year Ended 31 December 2022." https://www.nedbank.co.za/content/dam/nedbank/site-assets /AboutUs/Information%20Hub/Integrated%20Report/2023/Pillar%203%20Risk%20 and%20Capital%20Management%20Report%20for%20the%20period%20ended%20 31%20December%202022.pdf.

Otbasy Bank. 2022. "Annual Report '21: On the Way to Full Digitalization." https://hcsbk.kz /Otbasi_AR-2021_Book-Eng-.pdf.

SBG (Standard Banking Group). 2023. "Risk and Capital Management Report for the Year Ended December 2022." https://thevault.exchange/?get_group_doc=18/1680199049 -SBG2022RiskandCapitalManagementReport.pdf.

8 Third-Party Oversight and Competitive Neutrality

Baiterek is an unregulated financial holding company that owns several regulated financial subsidiaries. From a solvency standpoint, the Agency for Regulation and Development of the Financial Markets (AFR) supervises the Otbasy Bank, a second-tier bank, as well as the main legal entities of the agriculture complex (Agrarian Credit Corporation [ACC] and KazAgroFinance)—although these are not deposit-taking institutions and are therefore subject to a less demanding regulatory regime. Other entities in the group are subject to capital market regulation enforced by AFR. Crucially, two of the main credit entities of the group and systemically important lenders (financiers) in their respective sectors—the Development Bank of Kazakhstan (DBK) and the Entrepreneurship Development Fund (DAMU)—are neither regulated nor subject to prudential supervision.

The application of the rules defining banking groups could trigger the (mandatory) consolidated supervision of Baiterek Group by AFR. Baiterek should be identified as a financial holding company, effectively extending the scope of the regulation and supervision by AFR to the consolidated level. Capital, liquidity, corporate governance, or concentration requirements would be imposed at Baiterek's level in addition to the current applicable requirements to ACC, KazAgro, and Otbasy on a solo basis. Identifying Baiterek as the parent financial holding company of a banking group accurately reflects its operations. For example, Baiterek currently owns two Kazakhstani banks (Otbasy and Sberbank's former Kazakhstani subsidiary) whose subsidiaries engage in financial intermediation activities. For the definition of financial holding company and banking group, see BCBS (2023).

The potential privatization of Sberbank's former subsidiary (the Bereke Bank) will not change the arguments in favor of extending regulation and supervision to Baiterek on a consolidated basis. Under the current scenario, where Baiterek owns two of the largest systemic second-tier banks in Kazakhstan, this policy decision is admittedly more pressing. Nonetheless, if Bereke is finally privatized, Baiterek will still be the holding company of a large systemic bank (Otbasy) and other subsidiaries conducting financial intermediation at the Tier 2 level. The holding company will continue to provide financial intermediation for activities that are systemically important, such as agriculture, small and medium enterprise (SME) lending, and export insurance. Therefore, the case for consolidated supervision of Baiterek will continue to be strong.

Financial stability is another strong argument for extending regulation and supervision on a consolidated basis to Baiterek. First, Baiterek's consolidated assets are above 10 percent of Kazakhstan's gross domestic product and about 26 percent of total banking sector assets; these shares point to its systemic relevance. Second, the holding company has a key role in the provision of critical economic functions to Kazakhstani households and corporations. As mentioned above, Otbasy is the key player in mortgage lending to individuals, which raises significant questions about the substitutability of its functions—one criterion for locally systemically important financial institutions. As of 2023, Otbasy's deposit book covers a significant share of the Kazakhstani population. The agriculture subgroup provides critical economic functions to agricultural borrowers, who may find themselves experiencing financial problems if the activity of the group suddenly falters or stops. For some 40 percent of SMEs, access to external finance relies on Baiterek Group, particularly on DAMU. Furthermore, access to long-term finance for infrastructure and manufacturing for the Kazakhstani economy is provided by DBK. To a lesser extent, the provision of seed, venture, and private equity finance depends on the Baiterek Group and its subsidiary Qazaqstan Investment Corporation (formerly Kazyna Capital Management). Baiterek's size, the critical economic functions that it performs, and the doubts over the capacity of the Kazakhstani second-tier banks to step in and replace Baiterek or its parts are all strong arguments for reinforcing the regulatory and supervisory frameworks that are applicable to Baiterek.

Extending prudential supervision to Baiterek on a consolidated level will have several benefits. First, it will bring into the regulatory perimeter certain activities that currently have an outsized influence on Baiterek's risk profile—specifically those of DBK and DAMU. Furthermore, Baiterek's internal control functions and those of the unregulated institutions are likely to be significantly improved following the expected increase in the supervisory pressure that prudential consolidation will bring. Questions will be raised about the risk management tools, policies, procedures, and resources that Baiterek currently applies. Potential conflicts of interest that may emerge across the group will be highlighted. Furthermore, extending consolidation to the whole group can be a positive factor in enabling the group companies to raise funding (debt) or co-investment (equity) from the market. Consolidated supervision can help increase investor trust and credibility in the eyes of all stakeholders because most of the holding company's assets are currently excluded from prudential supervision.

Several arguments can be made against extending the perimeter of banking supervision, but they may not be valid or strong enough. First is the claim that capital, liquidity, and concentration requirements imposed at the consolidated level may restrict the financial capacity of Baiterek and its subsidiaries to provide financing to meet their mission and goals. In fact, most of these indicators have already been voluntarily adopted by Baiterek at the consolidated (and solo) level. Thus, they are likely suitable for ensuring sound capitalization, liquidity adequacy, and concentration limits at the group level. Another possible argument is that the financial and business autonomy of the regulated institutions (especially Otbasy) make consolidation superfluous. But a holistic view of the risks assumed by the group can hardly be considered as irrelevant—particularly given the presence of certain credit risks (for example, the exposure to second-tier banks across Otbasy, ACC, or KazAgro) and nonfinancial risks (for example, the possibility that subsidiaries' reputational and operational risks could affect Baiterek and other subsidiaries). Finally, it can be argued that Baiterek's state ownership and politicized corporate governance may render the AFR powerless to enforce new requirements. But this same argument does not support excluding state-owned banks from prudential supervision. Nor does the Basel III Framework include any exemption based on the ownership of the bank or financial institutions by the state (BCBS 2023).

The AFR could also extend its prudential supervision to DBK on a solo basis. The financial nature of DBK's risks (credit and financial risks) might already be a sufficiently strong rationale for subjecting DBK to banking supervision. Numerous development banks across the globe are subject to prudential supervision, both in developed and developing countries.[1] Some development banks are excluded from banking supervision, such as the Croation Bank for Reconstruction and Development, Vneshecombank in the Russian Federation, or the recently created British Business Bank. Remarkably, DBK is already expressing its risk appetite by employing the main regulatory indicators (capital adequacy, liquidity coverage ratios) and therefore implicitly assuming their effectiveness and suitability for monitoring its financial situation. Moreover, imposing prudential regulation and supervision on DBK could have several benefits: it could strengthen DBK's risk capacity and its self-sustainability, upgrade its corporate governance and transparency practices, reduce undue political interference in the bank, and focus more attention on environmental, social, and governance (ESG) and sustainability aspects.[2] It could also increase the transparency of its activities, especially against the backdrop of AFR's imposition of new prudential disclosures for second-tier banks. External prudential supervision could thus balance the pressure to provide more loans (at lower prices and longer terms) with closer risk management requirements. Nevertheless, some exemptions might be granted, considering the wholesale model and non-deposit-taking activities of DBK (Adams et al. 2022). Following other development bank models, DBK might be excluded from certain requirements, such as credit concentration limits or minimum liquidity requirements. Finally, it can be argued that, although DBK cannot be placed into regular insolvency proceedings, extending banking supervision to DBK could reduce the risk of losses and, therefore, better protect taxpayers' funds. For a thorough discussion of the rationale and implications of extending the regulatory and supervisory perimeter to public banks, see Adams et al. (2022) and Meyerhof, Palermo, and Gutierrez (2022).

The AFR, however, will not be in the best position to assess the compliance of Baiterek's subsidiaries with their development goals and missions. AFR is a prudential regulator and therefore specialized in the assessment of risks, internal governance practices, capital adequacy, and liquidity. Assessing compliance with development goals will be squarely out of the agency's current scope and capacity. Nevertheless, AFR can have an active role in ensuring that the Baiterek Group is actively assessing the climate and environmental risks (or more broadly, the ESG risks) that it may be exposed to. Sound management of these risks should be a priority for Baiterek, especially considering the role that the holding company's subsidiaries may have in channeling funds for climate change mitigation. Kazakhstan's commitments under the Paris Agreement and its efforts on climate change adaptation make Baiterek's financing role and market creation role potentially increasingly important.

Table 8.1 details the recommendations for Baiterek's third-party supervision and competitive neutrality.

TABLE 8.1 **Recommendations: Third-party supervision and competitive neutrality**

ACTION	RESPONSIBLE ENTITY	EXPECTED RESULT
Extend the regulatory and supervisory framework to Baiterek on a consolidated basis	MNE, MoF, AFR	Greater financial stability, sounder governance, and improved risk management for Baiterek
Refrain from excluding Otbasy from regulation and supervision	MNE, MoF, AFR	Financial stability; high standards for solvency, liquidity, governance, and risk management for Otbasy Bank
Consider extending regulation and supervision on a solo basis to DBK, with potential exemptions and carve-outs if justified by its mandate and activity	MNE, MoF, AFR	Financial stability; sounder risk management, solvency, liquidity, and governance standards for DBK; greater transparency in DBK's activities

Source: World Bank.
Note: AFR = Agency for Regulation and Development of the Financial Markets; DBK = Development Bank of Kazakhstan; MNE = Ministry of National Economy; MoF = Ministry of Finance.

NOTES

1. Developed country examples include KfW Development Bank in Germany, Caisse des Dépôts et Consignations in France, Cassa Depositi e Prestiti in Italy, Instituto de Crédito Oficial in Spain, and Banco Português de Fomento in Portugal. Developing country examples include Banco Nacional de Desenvolvimento in Brazil, Korea Development Bank in the Republic of Korea, Bank Gospodarstwa Krajowego in Poland, the Development Bank of North Macedonia, and the Development Bank of Bulgaria.
2. Around the world, prudential supervisors' focus on ESG and climate risk is encouraging banks to develop their sustainable finance capabilities.

REFERENCES

Adams, M. A., H. Y. Aydin, H. K. Choo, A. Morozava, and E. Sonbul Iskender. 2022. "Regulating, Supervising and Handling Distress in Public Banks." International Monetary Fund (DP/2022/010). https://www.imf.org/en/Publications/Departmental-Papers-Policy -Papers/Issues/2022/04/28/Regulating-Supervising-and-Handling-Distress-in-Public -Banks-511609.

BCBS (Basel Committee on Banking Supervision). 2023. "The Basel Framework." Bank for International Settlements. https://www.bis.org/basel_framework/index.htm.

Meyerhof, B., D. Palermo, and E. Gutierrez. 2022. *Application of the Key Attributes of Effective Resolution Regimes for Financial Institutions to State-Owned Banks.* Washington, DC: World Bank. https://elibrary.worldbank.org/doi/abs/10.1596/38111.

9 Transparency and Disclosure

This chapter is divided into three parts: The first reviews international experience and good practices related to transparency and disclosure in development finance institutions. The second section discusses major publications and information disclosure by Baiterek Holding and its subsidiaries, focusing on impact measurement. The third section presents recommendations to strengthen Baiterek's transparency and disclosure practices.

INTERNATIONAL EXPERIENCE AND BEST PRACTICES

The Organisation for Economic Co-operation and Development (OECD) guidelines on corporate governance of state-owned enterprises (SOEs) prompt SOEs to operate on the same principles as listed companies—namely, adherence to high-quality accounting, compliance, and auditing standards (OECD 2015). Major disclosures should include (i) financial and operational results and underlying activities carried out to support the public policy objectives; (ii) the governance, ownership, and voting structure of the enterprise, supplemented by a report on implementation of the corporate governance code; (iii) the remuneration of board members and key executives; (iv) fit and proper tests for board members, along with the process for their selection and their duties and responsibilities; (v) management of major risks; (vi) any direct or indirect financial support received from the government and affiliated institutions, plus any material transactions with the state and other related entities; and (vii) any relevant issues relating to employees and other stakeholders.

In 2020, OECD published a stocktaking report that evaluates the performance of national jurisdictions in implementing disclosure and transparency principles outlined in the guidelines (OECD 2020). In total, 27 jurisdictions self-reported their progress, and the report focused on SOEs (both financial and nonfinancial) operating in competitive markets and engaged in economic and commercial activities. The major findings of this report were as follows:

- *Almost all reporting jurisdictions apply the same disclosure requirements as private companies.* Several jurisdictions impose additional requirements, which in many cases cover public service obligations and reporting on funding and financing of noncommercial objectives. In most cases, legislation requires public disclosure, and noncompliance is subject to penalties. Adherence to these principles is summarized in panel a of figure 9.1.

- *The reliability and credibility of financial information disclosed by SOEs are highly dependent on the controlling environment.* First, the financial statements of SOEs should be prepared in line with international and national accounting standards. Second, financial statements should be audited by independent external auditors. Third, internal audits and controls should be organized in line with standards established by the Institute of Internal Auditors and other standard-setting bodies. Finally, the external and internal audits should be supplemented by regular state inspections. Adherence to these principles is summarized in panel b of figure 9.1.

- *Disclosures related to competitive neutrality are a key aspect of the government regulation of SOEs.* Among 27 reported jurisdictions, 15 require SOEs to disclose government financial assistance in their annual reports or financial statements. Belgium requires SOEs to report the legal basis, policy objective, form, dates, and total amount of financial assistance received from the state. Estonia and Israel not only impose reporting requirements but also disclose information on state assistance through dedicated registries or databases. The Transparency Act of Sweden requires SOEs to report on the use of funds provided by the state. In most countries, competitive neutrality reporting requirements are included in statutory laws related to competition, accounting, the securities market, and government aid, but in the case of Brazil, pertinent provisions are included in the Constitution.

FIGURE 9.1

International experience: Disclosures and controlling environment

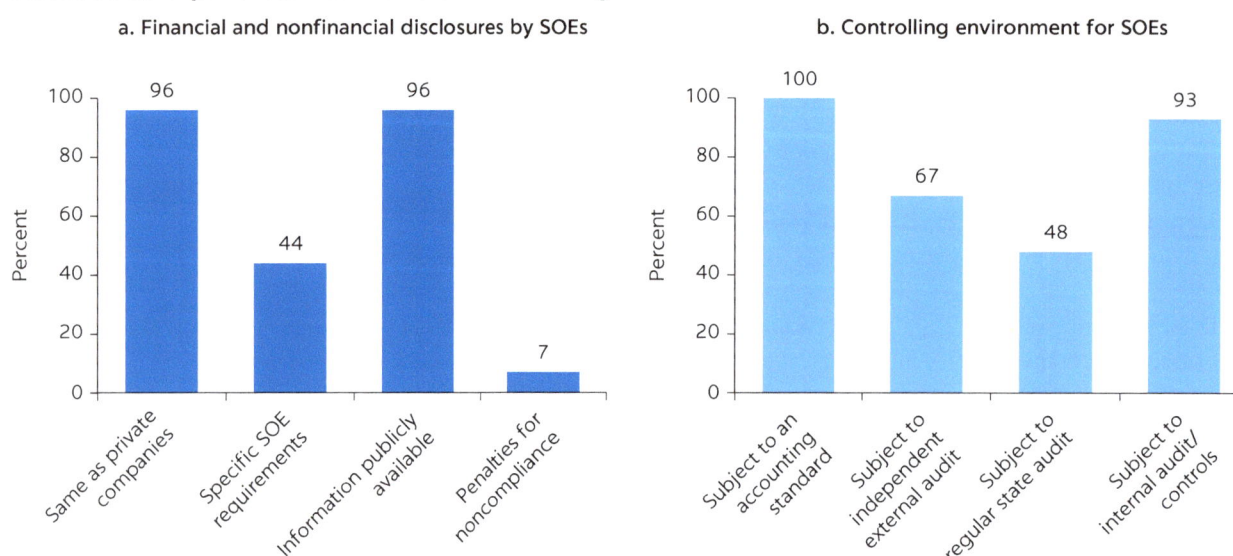

a. Financial and nonfinancial disclosures by SOEs

b. Controlling environment for SOEs

Source: OECD 2020.
Note: Note that (i) the sample included commercially oriented SOEs only; (ii) the reporting jurisdictions indicated that they require large, listed, and financial SOEs to follow the International Financial Reporting Standards (IFRS) or Generally Accepted Accounting Principles (GAAP); (iii) the independent external auditor requirement applies in Argentina to large, listed, and financial SOEs only, in Belgium and Japan to listed SOEs, in Costa Rica to financial SOEs, and in Germany, the Slovak Republic, and Türkiye to large SOEs; (iv) in 12 reporting jurisdictions, the state audit is performed on an ad hoc basis, a practice that is not welcomed by the guidelines; and (v) all reporting jurisdictions (except Hungary and Poland) lack specific requirements for SOEs regarding internal audit/control. SOE = state-owned enterprise.

DISCLOSURE AND TRANSPARENCY PRACTICES BY BAITEREK HOLDING AND ITS SUBSIDIARIES

In accordance with the OECD guidelines, Baiterek Holding and its subsidiaries prepare and disclose financial and nonfinancial information, but there is much room for improvement. General reporting includes, but is not limited to, annual reports, audited financial statements, and interim reports on operational and financial results. Baiterek's websites also provide information on corporate governance, including governance structure (organizational charts), board composition, board responsibilities and committees, senior management composition, major decisions by boards, and codes of ethics. However, information on nomination and selection of board members and senior management is scarce.

Baiterek discloses information relevant to competitive neutrality, but the level of disclosure varies across subsidiaries. In general, the holding company and its subsidiaries publish procurement guidelines, and in some limited cases they indicate actual implementation of these guidelines. Information on more important aspects of competitive neutrality, including financial assistance, regulatory exemptions, funding, and financial modalities, is scarce, and disclosure practices are not harmonized across subsidiaries.

Recently, subsidiaries of Baiterek have taken steps toward quantifying the development impact of their operations and disclosing impact measures to the general public. The reported measures attempt to quantify impact at both the macro and micro levels. In some cases, relevant reports also present information on the regional-level impacts. Moreover, several subsidiaries have tried to benchmark their operations to international peers. These disclosures of impact measurement and monitoring enhance the transparency of Baiterek's operations and are welcome. However, these efforts could be much improved, as highlighted in the following sections for several individual Baiterek subsidiaries—the Development Bank of Kazakhstan (DBK), Entrepreneurship Development Fund (DAMU), Qazaqstan Investment Corporation (QIC), and Kazakhstan Housing Company (KHC).

Development Bank of Kazakhstan

DBK publishes reports that assess its impact on the overall economy.[1] For example, a recent report analyzes macro-level effects of 293 projects implemented between 2017 and the first quarter of 2021. DBK collaborated with the Agency for Strategic Planning and Reforms (ASPIR), the Committee of Statistics, and the Ministry of Finance's Committee of National Revenue in publishing the report, which draws on information obtained from public sources and from clients of DBK, including information on sale revenues, export volume, new jobs created, and taxes paid. An underlying assessment methodology utilizes direct and indirect approaches; the latter approach relies on input-output tables. The report also aims at a quantitative breakdown of the impact by regions and major sectors of the economy. The report represents an important step in justification for DBK's operations. However, the underlying methodology has substantial room for improvement, especially its approach to quantifying DBK's economic additionality adjusted for the effect of confounding factors, and its identification and attribution of DBK's impact.

DBK also publishes reports of its impact on specific sectors of the economy. For example, a recent report discusses DBK's impact on the steel industry. The report presents valuable information regarding external factors affecting the sector, iron ore deposits in Kazakhstan, cost analysis of production, and key challenges faced by the steel industry. However, the report would benefit from more rigorous analytical methods, which would help to properly quantify DBK's impact on specific sectors of the economy.

DBK also publishes comparative analyses focused on its international peers. For example, a report published in 2020 compares DBK with similar institutions in Brazil, China, Ethiopia, France, Germany, India, Italy, Peru, Poland, and Vietnam. The report focuses on missions, strategies, financial indicators, and the macroeconomic environment where these institutions operate. However, the report is mostly descriptive; it could usefully analyze how to improve DBK's operations and organizational structure in line with international experience to deliver development and market creation impacts at an acceptable fiscal cost.

Entrepreneurship Development Fund

DAMU publishes reports showing its impact on the development of micro, small, and medium enterprises (MSMEs).[2] For example, a recent report by DAMU quantifies the macroeconomic impacts of its operations between 2014 and 2022, including effects on investment, employment, output, tax revenues, and credit portfolio composition of banks, and provides justifications for DAMU's operations using the dynamics of these indicators. But the report's approach to quantifying the impact of interventions could be improved. In the case of financial inclusion, the argument is based on aggregate changes in the credit portfolio of Tier 2 banks, but the counterfactual development, attribution issues, and effect of confounders are not properly addressed. The report could also benefit from recent developments in counterfactual analysis and synthetic control methods, which would allow it to properly consider any crowding-in or crowding-out effect at the level of financial intermediaries. The analysis needs to isolate the effect of different programs such as interest subsidies versus guarantees to improve attribution of impacts and avoid double or triple counting of impacts.

DAMU's reports also analyze its impact on regional development. These regional reports provide details on DAMU's interventions along with its key products, including guarantees, conditional placement of funds, and interest rate subsidies.[3] The main benefit of these reports is their identification of challenges faced by each region. For example, DAMU's recent report on the Kostanay region highlights inefficiencies in water and energy supply, lack of diversification (over-reliance on agriculture and extractive industries), and inadequate infrastructure (including roads that could provide access to markets). Another benefit of these regional reports is their assessment of trends in various sectors of the local economy and, most importantly, possible ways for DAMU to address challenges in the regions. However, they reveal little about DAMU's development impact on beneficiary MSMEs and the (positive) spillover on the MSME sector in the regions, or development of the local financial market (banks, microfinance institutions, investors) providing credit or equity to MSMEs.

DAMU also publishes reports on the gender impact of its operations. A recent report presents a basic analysis of the gender situation in the MSME segment, including the percentage of MSMEs and sectoral breakdown of businesses headed by women, and basic international comparisons with developed countries such as Canada, the Republic of Korea, and the United States. The report also presents gender coverage by the main products of DAMU, including guarantees, subsidized loans, and interest rates. Based on the report, 50 percent of projects supported by DAMU were related to female entrepreneurs; however, the monetary support (amount in tenge) was only 19 percent of the total support provided to MSMEs. These are useful output statistics, but they still offer little insight into outcomes: that is, they provide little information on the gender impact of DAMU operations, including the impact on the (increasing) presence of female-headed businesses in MSME loan portfolios of banks and microfinance institutions, based on a proper counterfactual and identification strategy.

DAMU's analytical reports also try to investigate the possibility of developing new products or expanding existing ones. For example, DAMU's recent reports analyze opportunities to develop leasing and factoring products that are at the early stages of development despite the high level of demand from MSMEs. The leasing market report is based on a survey of companies specialized in this market segment. The report shows dynamics and trends in the industry's assets, liabilities, and capital, and it also provides details on the structure of the leasing portfolio, the number of contracts signed, and the breakdown of the portfolio by major sectors of the economy. The report draws important conclusions by identifying major market players with which DAMU can cooperate in the future, and by quantifying the possible size and type of DAMU's intervention in the market. It rightly notes that the leasing market is dominated by quasi-fiscal institutions (they make up close to 95 percent of the leasing market), including Baiterek's subsidiary KazAgroFinance. Market gap assessments of DAMU and Baiterek in this area thus might focus on how Baiterek could help private institutions gradually replace the quasi-fiscal segment of the market by introducing more efficient and sustainable funding and operation mechanisms—notably through supporting risk-sharing products from Baiterek. Market gap analyses are useful, but more broadly, market gap analyses motivating Baiterek's interventions need to originate from a deeper understanding of business and financial risks and opportunities that MSMEs confront in different situations—industry, size, region, exposure to natural hazards, and so forth.

DAMU conducts customer satisfaction surveys among its clients. For example, a survey conducted in 2019 covered 620 entrepreneurs from three major cities (Nur-Sultan, Almaty, and Shymkent) and 14 regions. More than 90 percent of respondents expressed high satisfaction with DAMU's programs. In addition, close to 97.5 percent of respondents expressed their trust in DAMU. It is encouraging that the study was conducted by third parties not affiliated with DAMU, including experts from academic institutions. However, the credibility of the results could be improved if funding for such surveys came not from DAMU but from the institutions in charge of monitoring DAMU. It is also worth noting that close to 50 percent of DAMU's clients reported feeling frustrated by rather lengthy decision-making times, and more than 40 percent of respondents indicated they felt burdened by the number of documents required to process an application. These shortcomings could be addressed by undertaking the digital development of MSMEs, by including failed applicants for support in the pool of respondents, and by dividing customers by subsidies, credit lines, and partial credit guarantee support.

DAMU's analytical reports also cover specific thematic areas. For example, a recent report by DAMU investigated the possibilities of import substitution. DAMU's analysis identified products and services worth US$5.7 billion that could be subject to import substitution. In addition, the study quantified the probability of import substitution: 9 percent of products and services had low likelihood, 36 percent medium likelihood, and 55 percent high likelihood of import substitution. Future reports on import substitution could benefit from adopting more standardized methods of research, especially in relation to foreign trade, which could provide insights into the rationale for import substitution of specific products, given detailed analyses of costs and benefits. Overall, such broader economic studies might be outside the mandate of DAMU.

Qazaqstan Investment Corporation

QIC—formerly Kazyna Capital Management (KCM)—releases an annual sustainable development report that is now prepared in line with the Global Reporting Initiative standards.[4] The environmental component of the report has two sections: (i) QIC activities to reduce consumption of water and energy and reduce waste; and (ii) green projects financed by funds with QIC's participation. The latter include four renewable energy projects worth T 12.4 billion (US$28 million) with a total capacity of 200 MW. The social component of the report mainly focuses on internal issues such as employee benefits, education, safety, and health. This section of the report could thus be expanded to include an examination of social criteria related to other stakeholders, including customers, suppliers, and local communities. The governance component covers management structure; it deals with conflicts of interest and assesses the board of directors, compensation/remuneration policies, and procurement practices. The report also highlights QIC activities intended to address United Nations Sustainable Development Goals 3, 4, 5, 8, 10, 11, 12, 16, and 17. However, rigorous impact evaluations are still missing. If added, they would address issues of additionality (contribution), impact attribution, counterfactuals, and confounding factors.

Kazakhstan Housing Company

KHC's website hosts an analytical platform that provides detailed information about the housing sector of Kazakhstan. This platform is constructed using the Power BI tool, and it has dedicated dashboards with detailed information on construction companies, housing units, new construction, utilities available for housing units, price dynamics, and housing affordability. In addition, the platform provides information on socioeconomic indicators that are useful for housing market analytics, including total population, economically active population, migration statistics, the average size of households, and income and expenditures of households. Most of these indicators are represented by time series with regional breakdowns. By providing useful information to both households and construction companies, KHC is taking an important step in properly aligning the supply of housing units with the market demand. This information can help policy makers reach informed decisions about government subsidies and support. KHC needs to proceed to rigorous impact evaluations and reporting, including on end-beneficiaries (households demanding housing) and the mortgage loan market (private banks).

RECOMMENDATIONS

The scale and scope of Baiterek's operations offer the possibility of collecting large volumes of data on its clients and counterparts, including households, enterprises, and financial intermediaries. However, client-level data are not currently disclosed to stakeholders. Lack of data makes it harder for think tanks, researchers, and other independent groups to conduct analysis and impact evaluations of Baiterek's operations, thereby weakening its accountability and credibility. Data privacy legislation is often cited as a significant obstacle to data dissemination. However, data anonymization processes, including masking, pseudonymization, generalization, data swapping, data perturbation, and synthetic data techniques, can improve data transparency without violating privacy legislation; see the European Union's General Data Protection Regulation (EU 2016).[5]

Direct borrowing and contingent liabilities from quasi-fiscal activities affect debt sustainability. In recent years, Baiterek rapidly increased its liabilities by issuing bonds on the local stock exchange. The tapping of the capital markets reduced Baiterek's dependence on the budget, but at the same time, it amplified risks to debt transparency and sustainability. Quasi-fiscal activities, especially in the form of guarantees, also augment these risks if not properly managed and consolidated at the general government level. The debt management department of the Ministry of Finance in collaboration with the holding company should therefore seek to improve the production and publication of data on debt, guarantees, and other quasi-fiscal risks to sovereign debt that inform the decisions of strategic investors and government authorities responsible for public debt management and fiscal sustainability. It is crucial that this information be reflected in official policy documents such as the medium-term debt management framework and that it be disclosed to the general public—see, for example, IMF (2021) for recent developments in the debt sustainability framework for market access countries.

There is substantial room for improving the fiscal reporting framework, both on the Baiterek and the government side. For example, funds channeled through Baiterek for specific state programs should be clearly distinguished from the financial support directed toward Baiterek operations, including debt financing, subsidies, equity injections, and recapitalizations. The fiscal budgeting should consider a separate line for Baiterek, with breakdown by transfers and financing (loans, equity). In disclosing fiscal funding support, Baiterek Holding and its subsidiaries should more completely break down the support—into received transfers for subsidies to financial services, subsidies for own operations, transfers for performing the fiscal agent role; financing should be broken down in terms of loans, deposits, hybrid debt, equity, and dedicated financing for purchases of bonds from local executive authorities and other fiscal agency operations. The disclosure requirements, including formats, could be harmonized across all subsidiaries of Baiterek Holding, and drawing clear lines between fiscal and nonfinancial reporting would facilitate performance evaluations (Park 2021).

The impact assessment framework will be a crucial link between data production and dissemination. But there is substantial room to improve the framework for Baiterek by properly and independently evaluating impacts on jobs, value added, and environment. The independent impact evaluations should broaden beyond ultimate beneficiaries and include market creation aspects related to financial intermediaries and the market. This step would allow Baiterek to demonstrate that it does not operate on a "state forever" model and would also crowd in private capital and existing market segments in which private capital can take over financial service provision. For a review of impact assessment framework methods that can be adopted by Baiterek, see, for example, Cunningham (2021); Gertler et al. (2016); White (2009). Moreover, such independent evaluation should not be done by one selected entity—even if independent: all stakeholders should have access to adequate raw data, subject to anonymization and pseudonymization processes, to perform their own independent evaluation. To adhere to the best impact assessment practices, Baiterek should consider reporting data on its beneficiaries and participating financial institutions (PFIs) through the Bureau of National Statistics and the National Bank of Kazakhstan (NBK), or otherwise collaborate with the bureau to enable access to beneficiaries and matching nonbeneficiaries as well as PFIs and other financial institutions. This step would create proper pools of treatment and control groups and make it possible to rigorously evaluate the impact of Baiterek's interventions in the markets. Findings from various rigorous impact assessments should be considered and should inform Baiterek's supervisory board and senior management in their decision-making.

Data production and publication procedures should follow a standardized system to ensure comparability across different business lines of Baiterek. However, a certain level of flexibility should be allowed in order to account for project-specific circumstances and contexts. Generally, the standardized system should be based on detailed protocols that enable data sharing among key stakeholders—thereby ensuring transparency and accountability. These protocols should also provide clear guidelines on the planning, implementation, assessment, and dissemination stages. To ensure that the collected data will be utilized efficiently in decision-making, Baiterek should develop a theory of change, list key measurement indicators (such as country- and regional-level data on real incomes of individuals/enterprises, on employment, and on poverty, to name a few), justify its contribution, articulate how the attribution of market-creating and development impacts can be credible, and request that auditors include dedicated and sufficiently elaborate statements on the verified market and development impacts in the audited annual reports. The verification of reported impacts can be conducted regularly by specialized companies and periodically by the Auditor General Office (AGO) and/or ASPIR. It is important that the private impact verification companies are not paid by Baiterek but from independent financing sources.

Baiterek's data production and publication can be implemented in close collaboration with all stakeholders, including government organizations. Data production quality and consistency should be assured across different projects and target groups. Given the target groups' heterogeneity and the complexity of surveys/assessments, an independent organization with sufficient human resources and capacities should be mandated. The Committee of Statistics is a good candidate, given its experience in dealing with micro and macro data and administering household and enterprise surveys. Also, to ensure the relevance and comparability of collected data, it would be helpful to develop standardized templates of firm, household, and community questionnaires, as well as semi-structured interview topics; these could be developed to reflect the specific circumstances of Baiterek's subsidiaries—following the promising initiatives of DAMU. Regarding data on PFIs and Baiterek's impact on market creation in different segments of the financial system, coordinating with the NBK would be needed to ensure proper publication of data on the extent and nature of Baiterek's programs in which each bank and nonbank financial institution took part.

Baiterek's data and analysis should be disseminated effectively to all in a position to use them. Possible means of dissemination include publications, websites,

TABLE 9.1 **Recommendations: Transparency and disclosure**

ACTION	RESPONSIBLE ENTITY	EXPECTED RESULT
Enhance disclosures of client-level data, subject to proper anonymization and pseudonymization processes, and thereby allow stakeholders such as think tanks and researchers to conduct independent assessments, analysis, and impact evaluations of Baiterek's operations	Baiterek and subsidiaries	Enhanced market discipline and accountability
Improve production and publication of data on quasi-fiscal activities that pose risks to debt sustainability	MoF, Baiterek, and subsidiaries	Improved debt management framework and enhanced debt sustainability
Improve fiscal reporting framework where financing, subsidies, and fiscal agent money should be clearly distinguished	MoF/MNE and Baiterek	Improved fiscal transparency in relation to quasi-fiscal entities
Verify reported impacts through regular assessment by specialized companies and periodic assessment commissioned by AGO or ASPIR	Baiterek Impact Committee, AGO, Parliamentary Committee, ASPIR	Improved accountability for impact delivered by quasi-fiscal institutions like Baiterek
Enhance cooperation with third parties (such as the Bureau of National Statistics or NBK) specialized in macro- and micro-level data to improve cost effectiveness and outreach	Baiterek and subsidiaries	Reduced costs for data collection and availability for impact evaluations

Source: World Bank.
Note: AGO = Auditor General Office; ASPIR = Agency for Strategic Planning and Reforms; MNE = Ministry of National Economy; MoF = Ministry of Finance; NBK = National Bank of Kazakhstan.

and social media postings. Baiterek can also hold seminars and workshops to present its data specifics and discuss its analytical results with policy makers, project partners, and other stakeholders. Data analyses and impact assessments are likely to generate information that has value beyond the particular project assessed, and it is vital that the lessons learned be disseminated to all relevant stakeholders.

Table 9.1 summarizes the recommendations to improve transparency and disclosure related to Baiterek's operations; the ultimate goal is to enhance the institution's accountability for results, its market discipline, and the fiscal efficiency of its operations.

NOTES

1. Reports are available on DBK's website, https://www.kdb.kz/en/.
2. Reports are available on DAMU's website, https://damu.kz/en/.
3. DAMU also offers credit lines to its clients, and, as of December 2021, the outstanding unutilized balance was T 4.3 billion (approximately 1.1 percent of total assets).
4. The reports are available on QIC's website, https://qic.kz/en/.
5. For a recent review of anonymization techniques, see Goswami and Madan (2017); Majeed and Lee (2020); and Murthy et al. (2019).

REFERENCES

Cunningham, S. 2021. *Causal Inference: The Mixtape*. New Haven, CT: Yale University Press.

EU (European Union). 2016. "General Data Protection Regulation, Regulation (EU) 2016/679 of the European Parliament and of the Council." *Official Journal of the European Union*: L119/1–L119/88,https://eur-lex.europa.eu/legal-content/EN/TXT/PDF/?uri=CELEX:32016R0679.

Gertler, P. J., S. Martinez, P. Premand, L. B. Rawlings, C. M. Vermeersch, and M. J. Christel. 2016. *Impact Evaluation in Practice*. 2nd ed. Washington, DC: Inter-American Development Bank and World Bank.

Goswami, P., and S. Madan. 2017. "Privacy Preserving Data Publishing and Data Anonymization Approaches: A Review." *Proceedings of the 2017 International Conference on Computing, Communication and Automation (ICCCA)* (May): 139–42. doi:10.1109/CCAA.2017.8229787.

IMF (International Monetary Fund). 2021. "Review of the Debt Sustainability Framework for Market Access Countries." IMF, Washington, DC.

Majeed, A., and S. Lee. 2020. "Anonymization Techniques for Privacy Preserving Data Publishing: A Comprehensive Survey." *IEEE Access* 9: 8512–45.

Murthy, S., A. A. Bakar, F. A. Rahim, and R. Ramli. 2019. "A Comparative Study of Data Anonymization Techniques." In *Proceedings of the 2019 IEEE 5th International Conference on Big Data Security on Cloud (BigDataSecurity), High Performance and Smart Computing (HPSC), and Intelligent Data and Security (IDS)*: 306–09. doi:10.1109/BigDataSecurity /HPSC46356.2019.

OECD (Organisation for Economic Co-operation and Development). 2015. *OECD Guidelines on Corporate Governance of State-Owned Enterprises.* 2015 edition. Paris: OECD Publishing. http://dx.doi.org/10.1787/9789264244160-en.

OECD (Organisation for Economic Co-operation and Development). 2020. "Transparency and Disclosure Practices of State-Owned Enterprises and Their Owners: Implementing the OECD Guidelines on Corporate Governance of State-Owned Enterprises." http://www .oecd.org/corporate/transparency-disclosure-practices-soes.pdf.

Park, C. 2021. "Enhancing the Transparency and Accountability of State-Owned Enterprises." In *Reforming State-Owned Enterprises in Asia*, edited by F. Taghizadeh-Hesary, N. Yoshino, C. J. Kim, and K. Kim. ADB Institute Series on Development Economics. Singapore: Springer. https://doi.org/10.1007/978-981-15-8574-6_2.

White, H. 2009. "Theory-Based Impact Evaluation: Principles and Practice." *Journal of Development Effectiveness* 1 (3): 271–84.

Complete List of Recommendations

TABLE A.1 **Complete list of recommendations**

ACTION	RESPONSIBLE ENTITY	EXPECTED RESULT
Baiterek as a policy tool		
Update the mandate of Baiterek to include impact on ultimate beneficiaries and markets—including impacts on environmental outcomes—and additionality considerations in impact definition	Cabinet, MNE, Baiterek Board	More accountable impact framework covering climate change agenda
Abolish annual setting and negotiations of KPIs and targets for Baiterek; set the process on a four- to five-year cycle linked to MTEF; align KPIs with augmented/new mandate	Cabinet, MNE	KPIs aligned with augmented mandate and focused on medium-term impact; KPI targets more predictably linked to budget support/financing where needed
Review performance monitoring of Baiterek and its subsidiaries; allow for KPI hierarchy that also enables monitoring of performance at the level of Baiterek subsidiaries	MNE, Baiterek Board, AGO (and ASPIR)	Robust M&E framework established to assess performance of Baiterek at the subsidiary as well as group level
Review efficiency of the MNE oversight function and assess skill force needs and compensation policy for MNE ownership department	MNE	Enhanced MNE oversight capacity
Review Baiterek's pay scale to enable attraction and retention of talent from among financial sector professionals; consider comparability to NBK and AFR	Cabinet, MNE	Enhanced capacity of human resources to deliver on impact
Institutional arrangements and broader governance		
Develop ownership policy to define the rationale for operating a state-owned holding company of development finance institutions and to define the relation between state and Baiterek	Cabinet and MNE	Enacted ownership policy in line with best international practices
Revise performance contracts	MNE (and Baiterek Board and managers)	Improved performance and accountability of independent board members and professional managers

continued

TABLE A.1, *continued*

ACTION	RESPONSIBLE ENTITY	EXPECTED RESULT
Governance of Baiterek Holding JSC		
Reform board of holding company Option 1: Make the board of directors completely politically independent while raising the ownership unit to the level of the prime minister	PM and MNE	Adherence to OECD SOE corporate governance principles Full independence of holding company management and its insulation from political interference
Option 2: Change the composition of the board of directors so that independent directors become the majority	PM and MNE	Partial adherence to OECD SOE corporate governance principles Reduced political interference in holding company management while ownership and oversight functions are kept closer to holding company and subsidiaries
Include only independent directors in the specialized committees of the holding company's board	PM and MNE	Reduced political interference in holding company management
Conduct "fit, proper, and independence" tests of independent directors through a private international IDD company; cost of external IDD company should be considered as a regular budget expense of Baiterek	PM and MNE	Integrity of independent directors
Double bottom line and impact measurement		
For large investment projects, select projects based on maximization of ERR among mutually exclusive project alternatives, subject to a minimum IRR (hurdle rate)	Baiterek Board	Ensure alignment of investment projects financed by subsidiaries with development mandates with country's environmental and social objectives, including the Nationally Determined Contribution under the Paris Agreement
Estimate the ERR using the methodology of the World Bank (and other multilateral development banks) for economic analysis of projects, which is based on shadow prices, including the shadow price of carbon	Baiterek Board	Same as above
For small investment projects, select projects based on the maximization of economic and social impact using GIIN's IRIS+ impact measurement methodology; and/or make a selection based on ERR at the level of the investment program (rather than project)	Baiterek Board	Same as above
For all projects, calculate GHG emissions based on GHG Protocol Scope 2 (at a minimum)	Baiterek Board	Same as above
Baiterek subsidiaries' structure and governance		
Establish three subsidiary groups/corporations: • Commercialization and Privatization Group • Strategic Finance Group • Subsidy Management and Fiscal Agent Corporation	Baiterek Board	Alignment of subsidiaries' structure and management with their objectives
Establish a common board for each subsidiary group	Baiterek Board	Focus of board and management expertise on particular group objectives (commercial, double bottom line, subsidy)
Compose subsidiary group and corporation boards solely of independent directors	Baiterek Board	Political independence of subsidiaries' boards and management
Conduct "fit, proper, and independence" tests of subsidiary board members through private international IDD company	Baiterek Board	Integrity of subsidiaries' management

continued

TABLE A.1, *continued*

ACTION	RESPONSIBLE ENTITY	EXPECTED RESULT
Risk management structure and mechanisms		
Strengthen the risk management function at the Baiterek level, to ensure it has sufficient resources, stature, and expertise to undertake groupwide oversight responsibilities	Baiterek	Increase in risk management capabilities at the Baiterek level Reinforcement of corporate risk model
Upgrade Baiterek's internal audit function to a fully fledged group function, in part by amending its statute, reporting lines, and resources	Baiterek	Improvement in the internal control framework for Baiterek at the consolidated level
Create compliance monitoring units at Baiterek and its subsidiaries that partly replace the current internal control functions	Baiterek	Increase in the relevance of and control over compliance monitoring issues, including anti-corruption, greenwashing, AML/CFT, and data protection
Ensure that credit risk underwriting decisions are made at the DBK level and are free of political influence	Baiterek/DBK	Sounder credit risk underwriting standards, more free of conflicts of interests
Third-party supervision and competitive neutrality		
Extend the regulatory and supervisory framework to Baiterek on a consolidated basis	MNE, MoF, AFR	Greater financial stability, sounder governance, and improved risk management for Baiterek
Refrain from excluding Otbasy from regulation and supervision	MNE, MoF, AFR	Financial stability; high standards for solvency, liquidity, governance, and risk management for Otbasy Bank
Consider extending regulation and supervision on a solo basis to DBK and KHC, with potential exemptions and carve-outs if justified by its mandate and activity	MNE, MoF, AFR	Financial stability; sounder risk management, solvency, liquidity, and governance standards for DBK; greater transparency in DBK's activities
Transparency and disclosure		
Enhance disclosures of client-level data, subject to proper anonymization and pseudonymization processes, and thereby allow think tanks and researchers to conduct independent assessments, analysis, and impact evaluations of Baiterek's operations	Baiterek and subsidiaries	Enhanced market discipline and accountability
Improve production and publication of data on quasi-fiscal activities that pose risks to debt sustainability	MoF, Baiterek, and subsidiaries	Improved debt management framework and enhanced debt sustainability
Improve fiscal reporting framework where financing, subsidies, and fiscal agent money should be clearly distinguished	MoF/MNE and Baiterek	Improved fiscal transparency in relation to quasi-fiscal entities
Verify reported impacts through regular assessment by specialized companies and periodic assessment commissioned by AGO or ASPIR	Baiterek Impact Committee, AGO, Parliamentary Committee, ASPIR	Improved accountability for impact delivered by quasi-fiscal institutions like Baiterek
Enhance cooperation with third parties (such as the Bureau of National Statistics or NBK) specialized in macro- and micro-level data to improve cost effectiveness and outreach	Baiterek and subsidiaries	Reduced costs for data collection and availability for impact evaluations

Source: World Bank.
Note: AFR = Agency for Regulation and Development of the Financial Markets; AGO = Auditor General Office; AML/CFT = anti–money laundering and combating the financing of terrorism; ASPIR = Agency for Strategic Planning and Reforms; DBK = Development Bank of Kazakhstan; ERR = economic rate of return; GHG = greenhouse gas; GIIN = Global Investment Impact Network; IDD = integrity due diligence; IRR = internal rate of return; KHC = Kazakhstan Housing Company; KPI = key performance indicator; M&E = monitoring and evaluation; MNE = Ministry of National Economy; MoF = Ministry of Finance; MTEF = medium-term expenditure framework; NBK = National Bank of Kazakhstan; OECD = Organisation for Economic Co-operation and Development; PM = prime minister; SOE = state-owned enterprise.

Main Indicators for Baiterek Holding JSC

TABLE B.1 Main indicators for Baiterek Holding JSC

INDICATORS	2013	2014	2015	2016	2017	2018	2019	2020	2021	2022 (PRELIMINARY DATA)
1. Assets (T, billions)	1,865	2,325	3,460	4,103	4,433	4,719	5,214	6,813	9,870	12,232
2. Asset growth rate compared to the previous year (%)	—	25	49	19	8	6	10	31	45	24
3. Holding's consolidated assets as % of GDP	5.6	6	8.5	8.9	8.2	7.6	7.5	9.2	11	11.8
4. Liabilities (T, billions)	1,190	1,525	2,597	3,160	3,381	3,658	3,987	5,382	8,200	10,134
5. Liabilities growth rate compared to the previous year (%)	—	28	70	22	7	8	9	35	52	24
6. Net income (T, billions)	29	42	49	49	44	35	52	73	110.9	380.6
7. Retained earnings as a source of equity (T, billions)	—	—	—	36.8	97.2	81.8	142.9	196.8	175.8	524.7
8. Net income growth rate compared to the previous year (%)	—	141.4	118.7	98.3	89.8	79.7	148.4	141.8	151.8	343.2
9. Capital (T, billions)	675	800	863	943	1,052	1,061	1,227	1,431	1,670	2,098
10. Capital growth rate compared to the previous year (%)	—	19	8	9	12	1	16	17	17	26
11. Shareholder capital (T, billions)	633.1	718.3	758.3	802.3	846.2	846.2	917.2	1,046.5	1,266.2	1,366.2
12. Shareholder capital growth rate compared to the previous year (%)	—	13	6	6	5	0	8	14	21	8
13. Return on assets (%)	1.6	2	1.7	1.3	1	0.8	1	1.2	1.33	3.4
14. Return on equity (%)	4.4	5.6	5.9	5.4	4.4	3.3	4.5	5.5	7.15	20.2
15. Dividends paid (T, billions)	—	—	—	—	—	—	1.5	11.2	10.4	33.1
16. Number of subsidiaries in the structure of the holding company	10	11	11	11	11	11	11	9	8	8
17. Debt/capital ratio	1.8	1.9	3	3.4	3.2	3.4	3.2	3.8	4.9	4.8
18. Credit portfolio (T, billions)	849	1,361	2,126	2,390	2,603	3,102	3,633	4,282	6,166	8,160
19. Loans to business entities (T, billions), including	651.5	1,071.3	1,733.2	1,812	2,040.4	2,399.4	2,746.5	3,316.3	4,704.1	6,511.9
Corporate loans (T, billions)	549.6	989.1	1,541.9	1,568.2	1,626.5	1,614.7	1,584	1,816.7	1,806.3	1,741
20. Loans to banks and financial institutions (T, billions)	133.2	236.2	332.2	—	284.1	275.2	373.7	343.6	367.9	298.9
21. Mortgages and housing construction loans granted (T, billions)	61.2	—	—	—	243	360	527	609	1,235	1,382
22. Private capital as a share in the credit portfolio (%)	76.7	78.7	81.6	75.8	72	72.7	77.7	77.6	81.7	89.05

continued

TABLE B.1, *continued*

INDICATORS	2013	2014	2015	2016	2017	2018	2019	2020	2021	2022 (PRELIMINARY DATA)
23. Volume of long-term loans issued to large enterprises in non-primary sectors of the economy (T, billions)	81	251	262	278	422	443	453	486	533	358.9
24. Share of the holding company in annual long-term lending to large enterprises in non-resource sectors (%)	19	38	40	36	44	46	42	41	28	25.6
25. Loans granted to SMEs (T, billions)	—	—	—	—	549	495	611	1,680	2,197	1,554
26. Share of the holding company's loan portfolio (within the framework of direct lending instruments for SOEs) in the total volume of long-term debt of enterprises in non-primary sectors of the economy (%)	—	—	—	45	45	47.6	49.7	50.8	46.6	40.6
27. Share of credit portfolio and investment portfolio in total assets of the holding company (%)	47	61	65	71	69	73.2	78.2	78.5	73.64	74.4
28. Share of lending to SMEs with the assistance of the holding company in the total volume of long-term loans to nonbank legal entities (%)	—	—	—	30.5	40	37	48	41	40	32.7
29. Share of non-state sources of borrowing in the total structure of borrowing (%)	—	—	—	—	63	65.2	62.1	25.9	72.7	70.8
30. Total amount of issued guarantees (T, billions)	—	—	—	—	9.4	56.6	88.8	120.6	372	211.8
31. Bonds purchased of LEAs (T, billions)	—	—	—	38.2	71.8	98	108.8	281.2	163.7	176.4
32. Volume of insurance liability contracts (T, billions)	—	—	—	—	40	90	97	134.6	204.7	259.1
33. Trust index	—	—	—	—	86	87.8	88.1	88.3	87.5	87.2
34. Holding company total income (T, billions)	150.2	173.9	291.8	292	330	366.7	427	463	753	1,227
35. Holding company total expenses (T, billions)	111.3	122.3	215.2	254	278	314	363	378	610	846
36. Subordinated debt (T, billions)	17.7	14.2	14.7	15.2	5.4	6.5	6.1	7	7.5	8
37. Kazakhstan government's loans (T, billions)	60.9	61.8	54.4	103.6	180	208.8	283.8	347.7	577.4	776.6
38. Investment portfolio (T, billions)	23	48	139	517.7	450.1	350.7	442	1,067.7	1,102.3	1,024.5
39. Funds received from the state fund (balance to balance) (T, billions)	—	273	315.6	371.5	134.1	86.6	186.6	224.2	274.7	—
40. Issued debt securities (T, billions), including	344.6	505.7	800.4	1,026.3	1,126	1,439.8	1,649.6	2,511.2	4,065.4	3,739.5
a. Eurobonds (US$, millions)	279.4	331.3	526.4	469.2	468.8	529.4	534.5	557.2	791.5	394.1
b. Eurobonds (T, billions)	—	115.2	218	—	96.7	200	200.7	165	266.8	262.5
c. Mortgage bonds (T, billions)	49.9	47.9	39	29.8	35.2	38.6	44.9	30.6	60.9	61.3
d. Islamic bonds	10	11.3	16.9	15.9	—	—	—	—	—	—
e. Other bonds (T, billions)	5.1	115.2	215.8	511.3	525.5	671.8	869.7	1,758.3	2,946.2	3,016.5

continued

TABLE B.1, *continued*

INDICATORS	2013	2014	2015	2016	2017	2018	2019	2020	2021	2022 (PRELIMINARY DATA)
41. Loans from banks and other financial institutions (T, billions)	507.9	619.2	1,138	1,101.5	1,010.2	837.5	652.3	686.3	652.5	946.5
42. Government subsidies (T, billions)	—	—	—	—	—	411.2	456.1	580.1	741.6	1,052.5
43. Deferred income tax liabilities (T, billions)	0.2	7.1	26	26.2	28.4	19.4	26.2	33.7	40.3	45.3
44. Funds attracted through capital markets, by types of funds	—	3,164.6	2,608.4	3,057.4	3,194.4	3,432.2	3,663.9	5,063.1	7,181.3	7,825.2
a. US$, millions	—	4,765.5	4,787.8	4,600.4	4,190.7	3,317.4	2,807.3	2,853	3,109	2,431.1
b. Rub, millions	—	—	—	—	2,474	3,048	2,911	2,752.8	6,170	27,818.5
c. T, billions	—	713	983.1	1,524	1787	2,140	2,576	3,847.4	5,804	6,521.6

Source: Baiterek Holding.
Note: LEA = local executive authority; SME = small and medium enterprise; SOE = state-owned enterprise; T = Kazakhstani tenge (national currency); — = not available.

www.ingramcontent.com/pod-product-compliance
Lightning Source LLC
Chambersburg PA
CBHW041446210326
41599CB00004B/156